Power Through Prayer &
The Essentials of Prayer

Edward M. Bounds

Scibere Semper Et Legere

Contents

Power Through Prayer

The Essentials of Prayer

Power Through Prayer

— 1910 —

Chapter 1

Men of Prayer Needed

WE are constantly on a stretch, if not on a strain, to devise new methods, new plans, new organizations to advance the Church and secure enlargement and efficiency for the gospel. This trend of the day has a tendency to lose sight of the man or sink the man in the plan or organization. God's plan is to make much of the man, far more of him than of anything else. Men are God's method. The Church is looking for better methods; God is looking for better men. "There was a man sent from God whose name was John." The dispensation that heralded and prepared the way for Christ was bound up in that man John. "Unto us a child is born, unto us a son is given." The world's salvation comes out of that cradled Son. When Paul appeals to the personal character of the men who rooted the gospel in the world, he solves the mystery of their success. The glory and efficiency of the gospel is staked on the men who proclaim it. When God declares that "the eyes of the Lord run to and fro throughout the whole earth, to show himself strong in the behalf of them whose heart is perfect toward him," he declares the necessity of men and his dependence on them as a channel through which to exert his power upon the world. This vital, urgent truth is one that this age of machinery is apt to forget. The forgetting of it is as baneful on the work of God as would be the striking of the sun from his sphere. Darkness, confusion, and death would ensue.

What the Church needs to-day is not more machinery or better, not new organizations or more and novel methods, but men whom the Holy Ghost can use—men of prayer, men mighty in prayer. The Holy Ghost does not flow through methods, but through men. He does not come on machinery, but on men. He does not anoint plans, but men—men of prayer.

An eminent historian has said that the accidents of personal character have more to do with the revolutions of nations than either philosophic historians or democratic politicians will allow. This truth has its application in full to the gospel of Christ, the character and conduct of the followers of Christ—Christianize the world, transfigure nations and individuals. Of the preachers of the gospel it is eminently true.

The character as well as the fortunes of the gospel is committed to the preacher. He makes or mars the message from God to man. The preacher is the golden pipe through which the divine oil flows. The pipe must not only be golden, but open and flawless, that the oil may have a full, unhindered, unwasted flow.

The man makes the preacher. God must make the man. The messenger is, if possible, more than the message. The preacher is more than the sermon. The preacher makes the sermon. As the life-giving milk from the mother's bosom is but the mother's life, so all the preacher says is tinctured, impregnated by what the preacher is. The treasure is in earthen vessels, and the taste of the vessel impregnates and may discolor. The man, the whole man, lies behind the sermon. Preaching is not the performance of an hour. It is the outflow of a life. It takes twenty years to make a sermon, because it takes twenty years to make the man. The true sermon is a thing of life. The sermon grows because the man grows. The sermon is forceful because the man is forceful. The sermon is holy because the man is holy. The sermon is full of the divine unction because the man is full of the divine unction.

Paul termed it "My gospel;" not that he had degraded it by his personal eccentricities or diverted it by selfish appropriation, but the gospel was put into the heart and lifeblood of the man Paul, as a personal trust to be executed by his Pauline traits, to be set aflame and empowered by the fiery energy of his fiery soul. Paul's sermons—what were they? Where are they? Skeletons, scattered fragments, afloat on the sea of inspiration! But the man Paul, greater than his sermons, lives forever, in full form, feature and stature, with his molding hand on the Church. The preaching is but a voice. The voice in silence dies, the text is forgotten, the sermon fades from memory; the preacher lives.

The sermon cannot rise in its life-giving forces above the man. Dead men give out dead sermons, and dead sermons kill. Everything depends on the spiritual character of the preacher. Under the Jewish dispensation the high priest had inscribed in jeweled letters on a golden frontlet: "Holiness to the Lord." So every preacher in Christ's ministry must be molded into and mastered by this same holy motto. It is a crying shame for the Christian ministry to fall lower in holiness of character and holiness of aim than the Jewish priesthood. Jonathan Edwards said: "I went on with my eager pursuit after more holiness and conformity to Christ. The heaven I desired was a heaven of holiness." The gospel of Christ does not move by popular waves. It has no self-propagating power. It moves as the men who have charge of it move. The preacher must impersonate the gospel. Its divine, most distinctive features must be embodied in him. The constraining power of love must be in the preacher as a projecting, eccentric, an all-commanding, self-oblivious force. The energy of self-denial must be his being, his heart and blood and bones. He must go forth as a man among men, clothed with humility, abiding in meekness, wise as a serpent, harmless as a dove; the bonds of a servant with the spirit of a king, a king in high, royal, in dependent bearing, with the simplicity and sweetness of a child. The preacher must throw himself, with all the abandon of a perfect, self-emptying faith and a self-consuming zeal, into his work for the salvation of men. Hearty, heroic, compassionate, fearless martyrs must the men be who take hold of and shape a generation for God. If they be timid time servers, place seekers, if they be men pleasers or men fearers, if their faith has a weak hold on God or his Word, if their denial be broken by any phase of self or the world, they cannot take hold of the Church nor the world for God.

The preacher's sharpest and strongest preaching should be to himself. His most difficult, delicate, laborious, and thorough work must be with himself. The training of the twelve was the great, difficult, and enduring work of Christ. Preachers are not sermon makers, but men makers and saint makers, and he only is well-trained for this business who has made himself a man and a saint. It is not great talents nor great learning nor great preachers that God needs, but men great in holiness, great in faith, great in love, great in fidelity, great for God— men always preaching by holy sermons in the pulpit, by holy lives out of it. These can mold a generation for God.

After this order, the early Christians were formed. Men they were of solid mold, preachers after the heavenly type—heroic, stalwart, soldierly, saintly. Preaching with them meant self-denying, self-crucifying, serious, toilsome, martyr business. They applied themselves to it in a way that told on their generation, and formed in its womb a generation yet unborn for God. The preaching man is to be the praying man. Prayer is the preacher's mightiest weapon. An almighty force in itself, it gives life and force to all.

The real sermon is made in the closet. The man —God's man—is made in the closet. His life and his profoundest convictions were born in his secret communion with God. The burdened and tearful agony of his spirit, his weightiest and sweetest messages were got when alone with God. Prayer makes the man; prayer makes the preacher; prayer makes the pastor.

The pulpit of this day is weak in praying. The pride of learning is against the dependent humility of prayer. Prayer is with the pulpit too often only official—a performance for the routine of service. Prayer is not to the modern pulpit the mighty force it was in Paul's life or Paul's ministry. Every preacher who does not make prayer a mighty factor in his own life and ministry is weak as a factor in God's work and is powerless to project God's cause in this world.

Chapter 2

Our Sufficiency Is of God

THE sweetest graces by a slight perversion may bear the bitterest fruit. The sun gives life, but sunstrokes are death. Preaching is to give life; it may kill. The preacher holds the keys; he may lock as well as unlock. Preaching is God's great institution for the planting and maturing of spiritual life. When properly executed, its benefits are untold; when wrongly executed, no evil can exceed its damaging results. It is an easy matter to destroy the flock if the shepherd be unwary or the pasture be destroyed, easy to capture the citadel if the watchmen be asleep or the food and water be poisoned. Invested with such gracious prerogatives, exposed to so great evils, involving so many grave responsibilities, it would be a parody on the shrewdness of the devil and a libel on his character and reputation if he did not bring his master influences to adulterate the preacher and the preaching. In face of all this, the exclamatory interrogatory of Paul, "Who is sufficient for these things?" is never out of order.

Paul says: "Our sufficiency is of God, who also hath made us able ministers of the new testament; not of the letter, but of the spirit: for the letter killeth, but the spirit giveth life." The true ministry is God-touched, God-enabled, and God-made. The Spirit of God is on the preacher in anointing power, the fruit of the Spirit is in his heart, the Spirit of God has vitalized the man and the word; his preaching gives life, gives life as the spring gives life; gives life as the resurrection gives life; gives ardent life as the summer gives ardent life; gives fruitful life as the autumn gives fruitful life. The life-giving preacher is a man of God, whose heart is ever athirst for God, whose soul is ever following hard after God, whose eye is single to God, and in whom by the power of God's Spirit the flesh and the world have been crucified and his ministry is like the generous flood of a life-giving river.

The preaching that kills is non-spiritual preaching. The ability of the preaching is not from God. Lower sources than God have given to it energy and stimulant. The Spirit is not evident in the preacher nor his preaching. Many kinds of forces may be projected and stimulated by preaching that kills, but they are not spiritual forces. They may resemble spiritual forces, but are only the shadow, the counterfeit; life they may seem to have, but the life is magnetized. The preaching that kills is the letter; shapely and orderly it may be, but it is the letter still, the dry, husky letter, the empty, bald shell. The letter may have the germ of life in it, but it has no breath of spring to evoke it; winter seeds they are, as hard as the winter's soil, as icy as the winter's air, no thawing nor germinating by them. This letter-preaching has the truth. But even divine truth has no life-giving energy alone; it must be energized by the Spirit, with all God's forces at its back. Truth unquickened by God's Spirit deadens as much as, or more than, error. It may be the truth without admixture; but without the Spirit its shade and touch are deadly, its truth error, its light darkness. The letter-preaching is unctionless, neither mellowed nor oiled by the Spirit. There may be tears, but tears cannot run God's machinery; tears may be but summer's breath on a snow-covered iceberg, nothing but surface slush. Feelings and earnestness there may be, but it is the emotion of the actor and the earnestness of the attorney. The preacher may feel from the kindling of his own sparks, be eloquent over his own exegesis, earnest in delivering the product of his own brain; the professor may usurp the place and imitate the fire of the apostle; brains and nerves may serve the place and feign the work of God's

Spirit, and by these forces the letter may glow and sparkle like an illumined text, but the glow and sparkle will be as barren of life as the field sown with pearls. The death-dealing element lies back of the words, back of the sermon, back of the occasion, back of the manner, back of the action. The great hindrance is in the preacher himself. He has not in himself the mighty life-creating forces. There may be no discount on his orthodoxy, honesty, cleanness, or earnestness; but somehow the man, the inner man, in its secret places has never broken down and surrendered to God, his inner life is not a great highway for the transmission of God's message, God's power. Somehow self and not God rules in the holy of holiest. Somewhere, all unconscious to himself, some spiritual nonconductor has touched his inner being, and the divine current has been arrested. His inner being has never felt its thorough spiritual bankruptcy, its utter powerlessness; he has never learned to cry out with an ineffable cry of self-despair and self-helplessness till God's power and God's fire comes in and fills, purifies, empowers. Self-esteem, self-ability in some pernicious shape has defamed and violated the temple which should be held sacred for God. Life-giving preaching costs the preacher much—death to self, crucifixion to the world, the travail of his own soul. Crucified preaching only can give life. Crucified preaching can come only from a crucified man.

Chapter 3

The Letter Killeth

THE preaching that kills may be, and often is, orthodox—dogmatically, inviolably orthodox. We love orthodoxy. It is good. It is the best. It is the clean, clear-cut teaching of God's Word, the trophies won by truth in its conflict with error, the levees which faith has raised against the desolating floods of honest or reckless misbelief or unbelief; but orthodoxy, clear and hard as crystal, suspicious and militant, may be but the letter well-shaped, well-named, and well-learned, the letter which kills. Nothing is so dead as a dead orthodoxy, too dead to speculate, too dead to think, to study, or to pray.

The preaching that kills may have insight and grasp of principles, may be scholarly and critical in taste, may have every minutia of the derivation and grammar of the letter, may be able to trim the letter into its perfect pattern, and illume it as Plato and Cicero may be illumined, may study it as a lawyer studies his text-books to form his brief or to defend his case, and yet be like a frost, a killing frost. Letter-preaching may be eloquent, enameled with poetry and rhetoric, sprinkled with prayer spiced with sensation, illumined by genius and yet these be but the massive or chaste, costly mountings, the rare and beautiful flowers which coffin the corpse. The preaching which kills may be without scholarship, unmarked by any freshness of thought or feeling, clothed in tasteless generalities or vapid specialties, with style irregular, slovenly, savoring neither of closet nor of study, graced neither by thought, expression, or prayer. Under such preaching how wide and utter the desolation! how profound the spiritual death!

This letter-preaching deals with the surface and shadow of things, and not the things themselves. It does not penetrate the inner part. It has no deep insight into, no strong grasp of, the hidden life of God's Word. It is true to the outside, but the outside is the hull which must be broken and penetrated for the kernel. The letter may be dressed so as to attract and be fashionable, but the attraction is not toward God nor is the fashion for heaven. The failure is in the preacher. God has not made him. He has never been in the hands of God like clay in the hands of the potter. He has been busy about the sermon, its thought and finish, its drawing and impressive forces; but the deep things of God have never been sought, studied, fathomed, experienced by him. He has never stood before "the throne high and lifted up," never heard the seraphim song, never seen the vision nor felt the rush of that awful holiness, and cried out in utter abandon and despair under the sense of weakness and guilt, and had his life renewed, his heart touched, purged, inflamed by the live coal from God's altar. His ministry may draw people to him, to the Church, to the form and ceremony; but no true drawings to God, no sweet, holy, divine communion induced. The Church has been frescoed but not edified, pleased but not sanctified. Life is suppressed; a chill is on the summer air; the soil is baked. The city of our God becomes the city of the dead; the Church a graveyard, not an embattled army. Praise and prayer are stifled; worship is dead. The preacher and the preaching have helped sin, not holiness; peopled hell, not heaven.

Preaching which kills is prayerless preaching. Without prayer the preacher creates death, and not life. The preacher who is feeble in prayer is feeble in life-giving forces. The preacher who has retired prayer as a conspicuous and largely prevailing element in his own character has shorn his preaching of its distinctive life-giving power. Professional praying there is and will be, but professional praying helps the preaching to its deadly work. Professional praying chills and kills both preaching and praying. Much of the lax devotion and lazy, irreverent attitudes in congregational praying are attributable to professional praying in the pulpit. Long, discursive, dry, and inane are the prayers in many pulpits. Without unction or heart, they fall like a killing frost on all the graces of worship. Death-dealing prayers they are. Every vestige of devotion has perished under their breath. The deader they are the longer they grow. A plea for short praying, live praying, real heart praying, praying by the Holy Spirit—direct, specific, ardent, simple, unctuous in the pulpit—is in order. A school to teach preachers how to pray, as God counts praying, would be more beneficial to true piety, true worship, and true preaching than all theological schools.

Stop! Pause! Consider! Where are we? What are we doing? Preaching to kill? Praying to kill? Praying to God! the great God, the Maker of all worlds, the Judge of all men! What reverence! what simplicity! what sincerity! what truth in the inward parts is demanded! How real we must be! How hearty! Prayer to God the noblest exercise, the loftiest effort of man, the most real thing! Shall we not discard forever accursed preaching that kills and prayer that kills, and do the real thing, the mightiest thing—prayerful praying, life-creating preaching, bring the mightiest force to bear on heaven and earth and draw on God's exhaustless and open treasure for the need and beggary of man?

Chapter 4

Tendencies to Be Avoided

THERE are two extreme tendencies in the ministry. The one is to shut itself out from intercourse with the people. The monk, the hermit were illustrations of this; they shut themselves out from men to be more with God. They failed, of course. Our being with God is of use only as we expend its priceless benefits on men. This age, neither with preacher nor with people, is much intent on God. Our hankering is not that way. We shut ourselves to our study, we become students, bookworms, Bible worms, sermon makers, noted for literature, thought, and sermons; but the people and God, where are they? Out of heart, out of mind. Preachers who are great thinkers, great students must be the greatest of prayers, or else they will be the greatest of backsliders, heartless professionals, rationalistic, less than the least of preachers in God's estimate.

The other tendency is to thoroughly popularize the ministry. He is no longer God's man, but a man of affairs, of the people. He prays not, because his mission is to the people. If he can move the people, create an interest, a sensation in favor of religion, an interest in Church work—he is satisfied. His personal relation to God is no factor in his work. Prayer has little or no place in his plans. The disaster and ruin of such a ministry cannot be computed by earthly arithmetic. What the preacher is in prayer to God, for himself, for his people, so is his power for real good to men, so is his true fruitfulness, his true fidelity to God, to man, for time, for eternity.

It is impossible for the preacher to keep his spirit in harmony with the divine nature of his high calling without much prayer. That the preacher by dint of duty and laborious fidelity to the work and routine of the ministry can keep himself in trim and fitness is a serious mistake. Even sermon-making, incessant and taxing as an art, as a duty, as a work, or as a pleasure, will engross and harden, will estrange the heart, by neglect of prayer, from God. The scientist loses God in nature. The preacher may lose God in his sermon.

Prayer freshens the heart of the preacher, keeps it in tune with God and in sympathy with the people, lifts his ministry out of the chilly air of a profession, fructifies routine and moves every wheel with the facility and power of a divine unction.

Mr. Spurgeon says: "Of course the preacher is above all others distinguished as a man of prayer. He prays as an ordinary Christian, else he were a hypocrite. He prays more than ordinary Christians, else he were disqualified for the office he has undertaken. If you as ministers are not very prayerful, you are to be pitied. If you become lax in sacred devotion, not only will you need to be pitied but your people also, and the day cometh in which you shall be ashamed and confounded. All our libraries and studies are mere emptiness compared with our closets. Our seasons of fasting and prayer at the Tabernacle have been high days indeed; never has heaven's gate stood wider; never have our hearts been nearer the central Glory."

The praying which makes a prayerful ministry is not a little praying put in as we put flavor to give it a pleasant smack, but the praying must be in the body, and form the blood and bones. Prayer is no petty duty, put into a corner; no piecemeal performance made out of the fragments of time which have been snatched from business and other engagements of life; but it means that the best of our time, the heart of our time and strength must be given. It does not mean the closet absorbed in the study or swallowed up in the activities of ministerial duties; but it means the closet first, the study and activities second, both study and activities freshened and made efficient by the closet. Prayer that affects one's ministry must give tone to one's life. The praying which gives color and bent to character is no pleasant, hurried pastime. It must enter as strongly into the heart and life as Christ's "strong crying and tears" did; must draw out the soul into an agony of desire as Paul's did; must be an inwrought fire and force like the "effectual, fervent prayer" of James; must be of that quality which, when put into the golden censer and incensed before God, works mighty spiritual throes and revolutions.

Prayer is not a little habit pinned on to us while we were tied to our mother's apron strings; neither is it a little decent quarter of a minute's grace said over an hour's dinner, but it is a most serious work of our most serious years. It engages more of time and appetite than our longest dinings or richest feasts. The prayer that makes much of our preaching must be made much of. The character of our praying will determine the character of our preaching. Light praying will make light preaching. Prayer makes preaching strong, gives it unction, and makes it stick. In every ministry weighty for good, prayer has always been a serious business.

The preacher must be preeminently a man of prayer. His heart must graduate in the school of prayer. In the school of prayer only can the heart learn to preach. No learning can make up for the failure to pray. No earnestness, no diligence, no study, no gifts will supply its lack.

Talking to men for God is a great thing, but talking to God for men is greater still. He will never talk well and with real success to men for God who has not learned well how to talk to God for men. More than this, prayerless words in the pulpit and out of it are deadening words.

Chapter 5

Prayer, the Great Essential

PRAYER, in the preacher's life, in the preacher's study, in the preacher's pulpit, must be a conspicuous and an all-impregnating force and an all-coloring ingredient. It must play no secondary part, be no mere coating. To him it is given to be with his Lord "all night in prayer." The preacher, to train himself in self-denying prayer, is charged to look to his Master, who, "rising up a great while before day, went out, and departed into a solitary place, and there prayed." The preacher's study ought to be a closet, a Bethel, an altar, a vision, and a ladder, that every thought might ascend heavenward ere it went manward; that every part of the sermon might be scented by the air of heaven and made serious, because God was in the study.

As the engine never moves until the fire is kindled, so preaching, with all its machinery, perfection, and polish, is at a dead standstill, as far as spiritual results are concerned, till prayer has kindled and created the steam. The texture, fineness, and strength of the sermon is as so much rubbish unless the mighty impulse of prayer is in it, through it, and behind it. The preacher must, by prayer, put God in the sermon. The preacher must, by prayer, move God toward the people before he can move the people to God by his words. The preacher must have had audience and ready access to God before he can have access to the people. An open way to God for the preacher is the surest pledge of an open way to the people.

It is necessary to iterate and reiterate that prayer, as a mere habit, as a performance gone through by routine or in a professional way, is a dead and rotten thing. Such praying has no connection with the praying for which we plead. We are stressing true praying, which engages and sets on fire every high element of the preacher's being—prayer which is born of vital oneness with Christ and the fullness of the Holy Ghost, which springs from the deep, overflowing fountains of tender compassion, deathless solicitude for man's eternal good; a consuming zeal for the glory of God; a thorough conviction of the preacher's difficult and delicate work and of the imperative need of God's mightiest help. Praying grounded on these solemn and profound convictions is the only true praying. Preaching backed by such praying is the only preaching which sows the seeds of eternal life in human hearts and builds men up for heaven.

It is true that there may be popular preaching, pleasant preaching, taking preaching, preaching of much intellectual, literary, and brainy force, with its measure and form of good, with little or no praying; but the preaching which secures God's end in preaching must be born of prayer from text to exordium, delivered with the energy and spirit of prayer, followed and made to germinate, and kept in vital force in the hearts of the hearers by the preacher's prayers, long after the occasion has past.

We may excuse the spiritual poverty of our preaching in many ways, but the true secret will be found in the lack of urgent prayer for God's presence in the power of the Holy Spirit. There are preachers innumerable who can deliver masterful sermons after their order; but the effects are short-lived and do not enter as a factor at all into the regions of the spirit where the fearful war between God and Satan, heaven and hell, is being waged because they are not made powerfully militant and spiritually victorious by prayer.

The preachers who gain mighty results for God are the men who have prevailed in their pleadings with God ere venturing to plead with men. The preachers who are the mightiest in their closets with God are the mightiest in their pulpits with men.

Preachers are human folks, and are exposed to and often caught by the strong driftings of human currents. Praying is spiritual work; and human nature does not like taxing, spiritual work. Human nature wants to sail to heaven under a favoring breeze, a full, smooth sea. Prayer is humbling work. It abases intellect and pride, crucifies vainglory, and signs our spiritual bankruptcy, and all these are hard for flesh and blood to bear. It is easier not to pray than to bear them. So we come to one of the crying evils of these times, maybe of all times—little or no praying. Of these two evils, perhaps little praying is worse than no praying. Little praying is a kind of make-believe, a salvo for the conscience, a farce and a delusion.

The little estimate we put on prayer is evident from the little time we give to it. The time given to prayer by the average preacher scarcely counts in the sum of the daily aggregate. Not infrequently the preacher's only praying is by his bedside in his nightdress, ready for bed and soon in it, with, perchance the addition of a few hasty snatches of prayer ere he is dressed in the morning. How feeble, vain, and little is such praying compared with the time and energy devoted to praying by holy men in and out of the Bible! How poor and mean our petty, childish praying is beside the habits of the true men of God in all ages! To men who think praying their main business and devote time to it according to this high estimate of its importance does God commit the keys of his kingdom, and by them does he work his spiritual wonders in this world. Great praying is the sign and seal of God's great leaders and the earnest of the conquering forces with which God will crown their labors.

The preacher is commissioned to pray as well as to preach. His mission is incomplete if he does not do both well. The preacher may speak with all the eloquence of men and of angels; but unless he can pray with a faith which draws all heaven to his aid, his preaching will be "as sounding brass or a tinkling cymbal" for permanent God-honoring, soul-saving uses.

Chapter 6

A Praying Ministry Successful

IT may be put down as a spiritual axiom that in every truly successful ministry prayer is an evident and controlling force—evident and controlling in the life of the preacher, evident and controlling in the deep spirituality of his work. A ministry may be a very thoughtful ministry without prayer; the preacher may secure fame and popularity without prayer; the whole machinery of the preacher's life and work may be run without the oil of prayer or with scarcely enough to grease one cog; but no ministry can be a spiritual one, securing holiness in the preacher and in his people, without prayer being made an evident and controlling force.

The preacher that prays indeed puts God into the work. God does not come into the preacher's work as a matter of course or on general principles, but he comes by prayer and special urgency. That God will be found of us in the day that we seek him with the whole heart is as true of the preacher as of the penitent. A prayerful ministry is the only ministry that brings the preacher into sympathy with the people. Prayer as essentially unites to the human as it does to the divine. A prayerful ministry is the only ministry qualified for the high offices and responsibilities of the preacher. Colleges, learning, books, theology, preaching cannot make a preacher, but praying does. The apostles' commission to preach was a blank till filled up by the Pentecost which praying brought. A prayerful minister has passed beyond the regions of the popular, beyond the man of mere affairs, of secularities, of pulpit attractiveness; passed beyond the ecclesiastical organizer or general into a sublimer and mightier region, the region of the spiritual. Holiness is the product of his work; transfigured hearts and lives emblazon the reality of his work, its trueness and substantial nature. God is with him. His ministry is not projected on worldly or surface principles. He is deeply stored with and deeply schooled in the things of God. His long, deep communings with God about his people and the agony of his wrestling spirit have crowned him as a prince in the things of God. The iciness of the mere professional has long since melted under the intensity of his praying.

The superficial results of many a ministry, the

deadness of others, are to be found in the lack of praying. No ministry can succeed without much praying, and this praying must be fundamental, ever-abiding, ever-increasing. The text, the sermon, should be the result of prayer. The study should be bathed in prayer, all its duties so impregnated with prayer, its whole spirit the spirit of prayer. "I am sorry that I have prayed so little," was the deathbed regret of one of God's chosen ones, a sad and remorseful regret for a preacher. "I want a life of greater, deeper, truer prayer," said the late Archbishop Tait. So may we all say, and this may we all secure.

God's true preachers have been distinguished by one great feature: they were men of prayer. Differing often in many things, they have always had a common center. They may have started from different points, and traveled by different roads, but they converged to one point: they were one in prayer. God to them was the center of attraction, and prayer was the path that led to God. These men prayed not occasionally, not a little at regular or at odd times; but they so prayed that their prayers entered into and shaped their characters; they so prayed as to affect their own lives and the lives of others; they so prayed as to make the history of the Church and influence the current of the times. They spent much time in prayer, not because they marked the shadow on the dial or the hands on the clock, but because it was to them so momentous and engaging a business that they could scarcely give over.

Prayer was to them what it was to Paul, a striving with earnest effort of soul; what it was to Jacob, a wrestling and prevailing; what it was to Christ, "strong crying and tears." They "prayed always with all prayer and supplication in the Spirit, and watching thereunto with all perseverance." "The effectual, fervent prayer" has been the mightiest weapon of God's mightiest soldiers. The statement in regard to Elijah—that he "was a man subject to like passions as we are, and he prayed earnestly that it might not rain: and it rained not on the earth by the space of three years and six months. And he prayed again, and the heaven gave rain, and the earth brought forth her fruit"—comprehends all prophets and preachers who have moved their generation for God, and shows the instrument by which they worked their wonders.

Chapter 7

Much Time Should Be Given to Prayer

WHILE many private prayers, in the nature of things, must be short; while public prayers, as a rule, ought to be short and condensed; while there is ample room for and value put on ejaculatory prayer—yet in our private communions with God time is a feature essential to its value. Much time spent with God is the secret of all successful praying. Prayer which is felt as a mighty force is the mediate or immediate product of much time spent with God. Our short prayers owe their point and efficiency to the long ones that have preceded them. The short prevailing prayer cannot be prayed by one who has not prevailed with God in a mightier struggle of long continuance. Jacob's victory of faith could not have been gained without that all-night wrestling. God's

33

acquaintance is not made by pop calls. God does not bestow his gifts on the casual or hasty comers and goers. Much with God alone is the secret of knowing him and of influence with him. He yields to the persistency of a faith that knows him. He bestows his richest gifts upon those who declare their desire for and appreciation of those gifts by the constancy as well as earnestness of their importunity. Christ, who in this as well as other things is our Example, spent many whole nights in prayer. His custom was to pray much. He had his habitual place to pray. Many long seasons of praying make up his history and character. Paul prayed day and night. It took time from very important interests for Daniel to pray three times a day. David's morning, noon, and night praying were doubtless on many occasions very protracted. While we have no specific account of the time these Bible saints spent in prayer, yet the indications are that they consumed much time in prayer, and on some occasions long seasons of praying was their custom.

We would not have any think that the value of their prayers is to be measured by the clock, but our purpose is to impress on our minds the necessity of being much alone with God; and that if this feature has not been produced by our faith, then our faith is of a feeble and surface type.

The men who have most fully illustrated Christ in their character, and have most powerfully affected the world for him, have been men who spent so much time with God as to make it a notable feature of their lives. Charles Simeon devoted the hours from four till eight in the morning to God. Mr. Wesley spent two hours daily in prayer. He began at four in the morning. Of him, one who knew him well wrote: "He thought prayer to be more his business than anything else, and I have seen him come out of his closet with a serenity of face next to shining." John Fletcher stained the walls of his room by the breath of his prayers. Sometimes he would pray all night; always, frequently, and with great earnestness. His whole life was a life of prayer. "I would not rise from my seat," he said, "without lifting my heart to God." His greeting to a friend was always: "Do I meet you praying?" Luther said: "If I fail to spend two hours in prayer each morning, the devil gets the victory through the day. I have so much business I cannot get on without spending three hours daily in prayer." He had a motto: "He that has prayed well has studied well."

Archbishop Leighton was so much alone with God that he seemed to be in a perpetual meditation. "Prayer and praise were his business and his pleasure," says his biographer. Bishop Ken was so much with God that his soul was said to be God-enamored. He was with God before the clock struck three every morning. Bishop Asbury said: "I propose to rise at four o'clock as often as I can and spend two hours in prayer and meditation." Samuel Rutherford, the fragrance of whose piety is still rich, rose at three in the morning to meet God in prayer. Joseph Alleine arose at four o'clock for his business of praying till eight. If he heard other tradesmen plying their business before he was up, he would exclaim: "O how this shames me! Doth not my Master deserve more than theirs?" He who has learned this trade well draws at will, on sight, and with acceptance of heaven's unfailing bank.

One of the holiest and among the most gifted of Scotch preachers says: "I ought to spend the best hours in communion with God. It is my noblest and most fruitful employment, and is not to be thrust into a corner. The morning hours, from six to eight, are the most uninterrupted and should be thus employed. After tea is my best hour, and that should be solemnly dedicated to God. I ought not to give up the good old habit of prayer before going to bed; but guard must be kept against sleep. When I awake in the night, I ought to rise and pray. A little time after breakfast might be given to intercession." This was the praying plan of Robert McCheyne. The memorable Methodist band in their praying shame us. *"From four to five in the morning, private prayer; from five to six in the evening, private prayer."*

John Welch, the holy and wonderful Scotch

preacher, thought the day ill spent if he did not spend eight or ten hours in prayer. He kept a plaid that he might wrap himself when he arose to pray at night. His wife would complain when she found him lying on the ground weeping. He would reply: "O woman, I have the souls of three thousand to answer for, and I know not how it is with many of them!"

Chapter 8
Examples of Praying Men

BISHOP WILSON says: "In H. Martyn's journal the spirit of prayer, the time he devoted to the duty, and his fervor in it are the first things which strike me."

Payson wore the hard-wood boards into grooves where his knees pressed so often and so long. His biographer says: "His continuing instant in prayer, be his circumstances what they might, is the most noticeable fact in his history, and points out the duty of all who would rival his eminency. To his ardent and persevering prayers must no doubt be ascribed in a great measure his distinguished and almost uninterrupted success."

The Marquis DeRenty, to whom Christ was most precious, ordered his servant to call him from his devotions at the end of half an hour. The servant at the time saw his face through an aperture. It was marked with such holiness that he hated to arouse him. His lips were moving, but he was perfectly silent. He waited until three half hours had passed; then he called to him, when he arose from his knees, saying that the half hour was so short when he was communing with Christ.

Brainerd said: "I love to be alone in my cottage, where I can spend much time in prayer."

William Bramwell is famous in Methodist annals for personal holiness and for his wonderful success in preaching and for the marvelous answers to his prayers. For hours at a time he would pray. He almost lived on his knees. He went over his circuits like a flame of fire. The fire was kindled by the time he spent in prayer. He often spent as much as four hours in a single season of prayer in retirement.

Bishop Andrewes spent the greatest part of five hours every day in prayer and devotion.

Sir Henry Havelock always spent the first two hours of each day alone with God. If the encampment was struck at 6 A.M., he would rise at four.

Earl Cairns rose daily at six o'clock to secure an hour and a half for the study of the Bible and for prayer, before conducting family worship at a quarter to eight.

Dr. Judson's success in prayer is attributable to the fact that he gave much time to prayer. He says on this point: "Arrange thy affairs, if possible, so that thou canst leisurely devote two or three hours every day not merely to devotional exercises but to the very act of secret prayer and communion with God. Endeavor seven times a day to withdraw from business and company and lift up thy soul to God in private retirement. Begin the day by rising after midnight and devoting some time amid the silence and darkness of the night to this sacred work. Let the hour of opening dawn find thee at the same work. Let the hours of nine, twelve, three, six, and nine at night witness the same. Be resolute in his cause. Make all practicable sacrifices to maintain it. Consider that thy time is short, and that business and company must not be allowed to rob thee of thy God." Impossible, say we, fanatical directions! Dr. Judson impressed an empire for Christ and laid the foundations of God's kingdom with imperishable granite in the heart of Burmah. He was successful, one of the few men who mightily impressed the world for Christ. Many men of greater gifts and genius and learning than he have made no such impression; their religious work is like footsteps in the sands, but he has engraven his work on the adamant. The secret of its profundity and endurance is found in the fact that he gave time to prayer. He kept the iron red-hot with prayer, and God's skill fashioned it with enduring power. No man can do a great and enduring work for God who is not a man of prayer, and no man can be a man of prayer who does not give much time to praying.

Is it true that prayer is simply the compliance with habit, dull and mechanical? A petty performance into which we are trained till tameness, shortness, superficiality are its chief elements? "Is it true that prayer is, as is assumed, little else than the half-passive play of sentiment which flows languidly on through the minutes or hours of easy reverie?" Canon Liddon continues: "Let those who have really prayed give the answer. They sometimes describe prayer with the patriarch Jacob as a wrestling together with an Unseen Power which may last, not unfrequently in an earnest life, late into the night hours, or even to the break of day. Sometimes they refer to common intercession with St. Paul as a concerted struggle. They have, when praying, their eyes fixed on the Great Intercessor in Gethsemane, upon the drops of blood which fall to the ground in that agony of resignation and sacrifice. Importunity is of the essence of successful prayer. Importunity means not dreaminess but sustained work. It is through prayer especially that the kingdom of heaven suffereth violence and the violent take it by force. It was a saying of the late Bishop Hamilton that "No man is likely to do much good in prayer who does not begin by looking upon it in the light of a work to be prepared for and persevered in with all the earnestness which we bring to bear upon subjects which are in our opinion at once most interesting and most necessary."

Chapter 9

Begin the Day with Prayer

THE men who have done the most for God in this world have been early on their knees. He who fritters away the early morning, its opportunity and freshness, in other pursuits than seeking God will make poor headway seeking him the rest of the day. If God is not first in our thoughts and efforts in the morning, he will be in the last place the remainder of the day.

Behind this early rising and early praying is the ardent desire which presses us into this pursuit after God. Morning listlessness is the index to a listless heart. The heart which is behindhand in seeking God in the morning has lost its relish for God. David's heart was ardent after God. He hungered and thirsted after God, and so he sought God early, before daylight. The bed and sleep could not chain

43

his soul in its eagerness after God. Christ longed for communion with God; and so, rising a great while before day, he would go out into the mountain to pray. The disciples, when fully awake and ashamed of their indulgence, would know where to find him. We might go through the list of men who have mightily impressed the world for God, and we would find them early after God.

A desire for God which cannot break the chains of sleep is a weak thing and will do but little good for God after it has indulged itself fully. The desire for God that keeps so far behind the devil and the world at the beginning of the day will never catch up.

It is not simply the getting up that puts men to the front and makes them captain generals in God's hosts, but it is the ardent desire which stirs and breaks all self-indulgent chains. But the getting up gives vent, increase, and strength to the desire. If they had lain in bed and indulged themselves, the desire would have been quenched. The desire aroused them and put them on the stretch for God, and this heeding and acting on the call gave their faith its grasp on God and gave to their hearts the sweetest and fullest revelation of God, and this strength of faith and fullness of revelation made them saints by eminence, and the halo of their saint-hood has come down to us, and we have entered on the enjoyment of their conquests. But we take our fill in enjoyment, and not in productions. We build their tombs and write their epitaphs, but are careful not to follow their examples.

We need a generation of preachers who seek God and seek him early, who give the freshness and dew of effort to God, and secure in return the freshness and fullness of his power that he may be as the dew to them, full of gladness and strength, through all the heat and labor of the day. Our laziness after God is our crying sin. The children of this world are far wiser than we. They are at it early and late. We do not seek God with ardor and diligence. No man gets God who does not follow hard after him, and no soul follows hard after God who is not after him in early morn.

Chapter 10

Prayer and Devotion United

NEVER was there greater need for saintly men and women; more imperative still is the call for saintly, God-devoted preachers. The world moves with gigantic strides. Satan has his hold and rule on the world, and labors to make all its movements subserve his ends. Religion must do its best work, present its most attractive and perfect models. By every means, modern sainthood must be inspired by the loftiest ideals and by the largest possibilities through the Spirit. Paul lived on his knees, that the Ephesian Church might measure the heights, breadths, and depths of an unmeasurable saintliness, and "be filled with all the fullness of God." Epaphras laid himself out with the exhaustive toil and strenuous conflict of fervent prayer, that the Colossian Church might "stand perfect and complete in all the will of God." Everywhere, everything in apostolic times was on the stretch that the people of God might each and "all come in the unity of the faith, and of the knowledge of the Son of God, unto a perfect man, unto the measure of the stature of the fullness of Christ." No premium was given to dwarfs; no encouragement to an old babyhood. The babies were to grow; the old, instead of feebleness and infirmities, were to bear fruit in old age, and be fat and flourishing. The divinest thing in religion is holy men and holy women.

No amount of money, genius, or culture can move things for God. Holiness energizing the soul, the whole man aflame with love, with desire for more faith, more prayer, more zeal, more consecration—this is the secret of power. These we need and must have, and men must be the incarnation of this God-inflamed devotedness. God's advance has been stayed, his cause crippled: his name dishonored for their lack. Genius (though the loftiest and most gifted), education (though the most learned and refined), position, dignity, place, honored names, high ecclesiastics cannot move this chariot of our God. It is a fiery one, and fiery forces only can move it. The genius of a Milton fails. The imperial strength of a Leo fails. Brainerd's spirit can move it. Brainerd's spirit was on fire for God, on fire for souls. Nothing earthly, worldly, selfish came in to abate in the least the intensity of this all-impelling and all-consuming force and flame.

Prayer is the creator as well as the channel of devotion. The spirit of devotion is the spirit of prayer. Prayer and devotion are united as soul and body are united, as life and the heart are united. There is no real prayer without devotion, no devotion without prayer. The preacher must be surrendered to God in the holiest devotion. He is not a professional man, his ministry is not a profession; it is a divine institution, a divine devotion. He is devoted to God. His aim, aspirations, ambition are for God and to God, and to such prayer is as essential as food is to life.

The preacher, above everything else, must be devoted to God. The preacher's relations to God are the insignia and credentials of his ministry. These must be clear, conclusive, unmistakable. No common, surface type of piety must be his. If he does not excel in grace, he does not excel at all. If he does not preach by life, character, conduct, he does not preach at all. If his piety be light, his preaching may be as soft and as sweet as music, as gifted as Apollo, yet its weight will be a feather's weight, visionary, fleeting as the morning cloud or the early dew. Devotion to God—there is no substitute for this in the preacher's character and conduct. Devotion to a Church, to opinions, to an organization, to orthodoxy—these are paltry, misleading, and vain when they become the source of inspiration, the animus of a call. God must be the mainspring of the preacher's effort, the fountain and crown of all his toil. The name and honor of Jesus Christ, the advance of his cause, must be all in all. The preacher must have no inspiration but the name of Jesus Christ, no ambition but to have him glorified, no toil but for him. Then prayer will be a source of his illuminations, the means of perpetual advance, the gauge of his success. The perpetual aim, the only ambition, the preacher can cherish is to have God with him.

Never did the cause of God need perfect illustrations of the possibilities of prayer more than in this age. No age, no person, will be ensamples of the gospel power except the ages or persons of deep and earnest prayer. A prayerless age will have but scant models of divine power. Prayerless hearts will never rise to these Alpine heights. The age may be a better age than the past, but there is an infinite distance between the betterment of an age by the force of an advancing civilization and its betterment by the increase of holiness and Christlikeness by the energy of prayer. The Jews were much better when Christ came than in the ages before. It was the golden age of their Pharisaic religion. Their golden religious age crucified Christ. Never more praying, never less praying; never more sacrifices, never less sacrifice; never less idolatry, never more idolatry;

never more of temple worship, never less of God worship; never more of lip service, never less of heart service (God worshiped by lips whose hearts and hands crucified God's Son!); never more of churchgoers, never less of saints.

It is prayer-force which makes saints. Holy characters are formed by the power of real praying. The more of true saints, the more of praying; the more of praying, the more of true saints.

Chapter 11

An Example of Devotion

GOD has now, and has had, many of these devoted, prayerful preachers—men in whose lives prayer has been a mighty, controlling, conspicuous force. The world has felt their power, God has felt and honored their power, God's cause has moved mightily and swiftly by their prayers, holiness has shone out in their characters with a divine effulgence.

God found one of the men he was looking for in David Brainerd, whose work and name have gone into history. He was no ordinary man, but was capable of shining in any company, the peer of the wise and gifted ones, eminently suited to fill the most attractive pulpits and to labor among the most refined and the cultured, who were so anxious to secure him for their pastor. President Edwards bears testimony that he was "a young man of distin-gushed talents, had extraordinary knowledge of men and things, had rare conversational powers, ex-celled in his knowledge of theology, and was truly, for one so young, an extraordinary divine, and espe-cially in all matters relating to experimental reli-gion. I never knew his equal of his age and standing for clear and accurate notions of the nature and es-sence of true religion. His manner in prayer was al-most inimitable, such as I have very rarely known equaled. His learning was very considerable, and he had extraordinary gifts for the pulpit."

No sublimer story has been recorded in earthly annals than that of David Brainerd; no miracle at-tests with diviner force the truth of Christianity than the life and work of such a man. Alone in the savage wilds of America, struggling day and night with a mortal disease, unschooled in the care of souls, having access to the Indians for a large por-tion of time only through the bungling medium of a pagan interpreter, with the Word of God in his heart and in his hand, his soul fired with the divine flame, a place and time to pour out his soul to God in prayer, he fully established the worship of God and secured all its gracious results. The Indians were changed with a great change from the lowest besotments of an ignorant and debased heathenism to pure, devout, intelligent Christians; all vice re-formed, the external duties of Christianity at once embraced and acted on; family prayer set up; the Sabbath instituted and religiously observed; the internal graces of religion exhibited with growing sweetness and strength. The solution of these results is found in David Brainerd himself, not in the conditions or accidents but in the man Brainerd. He was God's man, for God first and last and all the time. God could flow unhindered through him. The omnipotence of grace was neither arrested nor straightened by the conditions of his heart; the whole channel was broadened and cleaned out for God's fullest and most powerful passage, so that God with all his mighty forces could come down on the hopeless, savage wilderness, and transform it into his blooming and fruitful garden; for nothing is too hard for God to do if he can get the right kind of a man to do it with.

Brainerd lived the life of holiness and prayer. His diary is full and monotonous with the record of his seasons of fasting, meditation, and retirement. The time he spent in private prayer amounted to many hours daily. "When I return home," he said, "and give myself to meditation, prayer, and fasting, my soul longs for mortification, self-denial, humility, and divorcement from all things of the world." "I have nothing to do," he said, "with earth but only to labor in it honestly for God. I do not desire to live one minute for anything which earth can afford." After this high order did he pray: "Feeling somewhat of the sweetness of communion with God and the constraining force of his love, and how admirably it captivates the soul and makes all the desires and affections to center in God, I set apart this day for secret fasting and prayer, to entreat God to direct and bless me with regard to the great work which I have in view of preaching the gospel, and that the Lord would return to me and show me the light of his countenance. I had little life and power in the forenoon. Near the middle of the afternoon God enabled me to wrestle ardently in intercession for my absent friends, but just at night the Lord visited me marvelously in prayer. I think my soul was never in such agony before. I felt no restraint, for the treasures of divine grace were opened to me. I wrestled for absent friends, for the ingathering of souls, for multitudes of poor souls, and for many that I thought were the children of God, personally, in many distant places. I was in such agony from sun half an hour high till near dark that I was all over wet with sweat, but yet it seemed to me I had done nothing. O, my dear Saviour did sweat blood for poor souls! I longed for more compassion toward them. I felt still in a sweet frame, under a sense of divine love and grace, and went to bed in such a frame, with my heart set on God." It was prayer which gave to his life and ministry their marvelous power.

The men of mighty prayer are men of spiritual

might. Prayers never die. Brainerd's whole life was a life of prayer. By day and by night he prayed. Before preaching and after preaching he prayed. Riding through the interminable solitudes of the forests he prayed. On his bed of straw he prayed. Retiring to the dense and lonely forests, he prayed. Hour by hour, day after day, early morn and late at night, he was praying and fasting, pouring out his soul, interceding, communing with God. He was with God mightily in prayer, and God was with him mightily, and by it he being dead yet speaketh and worketh, and will speak and work till the end comes, and among the glorious ones of that glorious day he will be with the first.

Jonathan Edwards says of him: "His life shows the right way to success in the works of the ministry. He sought it as the soldier seeks victory in a siege or battle; or as a man that runs a race for a great prize. Animated with love to Christ and souls, how did he labor? Always fervently. Not only in word and doctrine, in public and in private, but in prayers by day and night, wrestling with God in secret and travailing in birth with unutterable groans and agonies, until Christ was formed in the hearts of the people to whom he was sent. Like a true son of Jacob, he persevered in wrestling through all the darkness of the night, until the breaking of the day!"

Chapter 12

Heart Preparation Necessary

PRAYER, with its manifold and many-sided forces, helps the mouth to utter the truth in its fullness and freedom. The preacher is to be prayed for, the preacher is made by prayer. The preacher's mouth is to be prayed for; his mouth is to be opened and filled by prayer. A holy mouth is made by praying, by much praying; a brave mouth is made by praying, by much praying. The Church and the world, God and heaven, owe much to Paul's mouth; Paul's mouth owed its power to prayer.

How manifold, illimitable, valuable, and helpful prayer is to the preacher in so many ways, at so many points, in every way! One great value is, it helps his heart.

Praying makes the preacher a heart preacher. Prayer puts the preacher's heart into the preacher's sermon; prayer puts the preacher's sermon into the preacher's heart.

The heart makes the preacher. Men of great hearts are great preachers. Men of bad hearts may do a measure of good, but this is rare. The hireling and the stranger may help the sheep at some points, but it is the good shepherd with the good shepherd's heart who will bless the sheep and answer the full measure of the shepherd's place.

We have emphasized sermon-preparation until we have lost sight of the important thing to be prepared—the heart. A prepared heart is much better than a prepared sermon. A prepared heart will make a prepared sermon.

Volumes have been written laying down the mechanics and taste of sermon-making, until we have become possessed with the idea that this scaffolding is the building. The young preacher has been taught to lay out all his strength on the form, taste, and beauty of his sermon as a mechanical and intellectual product. We have thereby cultivated a vicious taste among the people and raised the clamor for talent instead of grace, eloquence instead of piety, rhetoric instead of revelation, reputation and brilliancy instead of holiness. By it we have lost the true idea of preaching, lost preaching power, lost pungent conviction for sin, lost the rich experience and elevated Christian character, lost the authority over consciences and lives which always results from genuine preaching.

It would not do to say that preachers study too much. Some of them do not study at all; others do not study enough. Numbers do not study the right way to show themselves workmen approved of God. But our great lack is not in head culture, but in heart culture; not lack of knowledge but lack of holiness is our sad and telling defect—not that we know too much, but that we do not meditate on God and his word and watch and fast and pray enough. The heart is the great hindrance to our preaching. Words pregnant with divine truth find in our hearts nonconductors; arrested, they fall shorn and powerless.

Can ambition, that lusts after praise and place, preach the gospel of Him who made himself of no reputation and took on Him the form of a servant? Can the proud, the vain, the egotistical preach the gospel of him who was meek and lowly? Can the bad-tempered, passionate, selfish, hard, worldly man preach the system which teems with long-suffering, self-denial, tenderness, which imperatively demands separation from enmity and crucifixion to the world? Can the hireling official, heartless, perfunctory, preach the gospel which demands the shepherd to give his life for the sheep? Can the covetous man, who counts salary and money, preach the gospel till he has gleaned his heart and can say in the spirit of Christ and Paul in the words of Wesley: "I count it dung and dross; I trample it under my feet; I (yet not I, but the grace of God in me) esteem it just as the mire of the streets, I desire it not, I seek it not?" God's revelation does not need the light of human genius, the polish and strength of human culture, the brilliancy of human thought, the force of human brains to adorn or enforce it; but it does demand the simplicity, the docility, humility, and faith of a child's heart.

It was this surrender and subordination of intellect and genius to the divine and spiritual forces which made Paul peerless among the apostles. It was this which gave Wesley his power and radicated his labors in the history of humanity. This gave to Loyola the strength to arrest the retreating forces of Catholicism.

Our great need is heart-preparation. Luther held it as an axiom: "He who has prayed well has studied well." We do not say that men are not to think and use their intellects; but he will use his intellect best who cultivates his heart most. We do not say that preachers should not be students; but we do say that their great study should be the Bible, and he studies the Bible best who has kept his heart with diligence. We do not say that the preacher should not know men, but he will be the greater adept in human nature who has fathomed the depths and intricacies of his own heart. We do say that while the channel of preaching is the mind, its fountain is the heart; you may broaden and deepen the channel, but if you do not look well to the purity and depth of the fountain, you will have a dry or polluted channel. We do say that almost any man of common intelligence has sense enough to preach the gospel, but very few have grace enough to do so. We do say that he who has struggled with his own heart and conquered it; who has taught it humility, faith, love, truth, mercy, sympathy, courage; who can pour the rich treasures of the heart thus trained, through a manly intellect, all surcharged with the power of the gospel on the consciences of his hearers—such a one will be the truest, most successful preacher in the esteem of his Lord.

Chapter 13

Grace from the Heart Rather than the Head

THE heart is the Saviour of the world. Heads do not save. Genius, brains, brilliancy, strength, natural gifts do not save. The gospel flows through hearts. All the mightiest forces are heart forces. All the sweetest and loveliest graces are heart graces. Great hearts make great characters; great hearts make divine characters. God is love. There is nothing greater than love, nothing greater than God. Hearts make heaven; heaven is love. There is nothing higher, nothing sweeter, than heaven. It is the heart and not the head which makes God's great preachers. The heart counts much every way in religion. The heart must speak from the pulpit. The heart must hear in the pew. In fact, we serve God with our hearts. Head homage does not pass current in heaven.

We believe that one of the serious and most popular errors of the modern pulpit is the putting of more thought than prayer, of more head than of heart in its sermons. Big hearts make big preachers; good hearts make good preachers. A theological school to enlarge and cultivate the heart is the golden desideratum of the gospel. The pastor binds his people to him and rules his people by his heart. They may admire his gifts, they may be proud of his ability, they may be affected for the time by his sermons; but the stronghold of his power is his heart. His scepter is love. The throne of his power is his heart.

The good shepherd gives his life for the sheep. Heads never make martyrs. It is the heart which surrenders the life to love and fidelity. It takes great courage to be a faithful pastor, but the heart alone can supply this courage. Gifts and genius may be brave, but it is the gifts and genius of the heart and not of the head.

It is easier to fill the head than it is to prepare the heart. It is easier to make a brain sermon than a heart sermon. It was heart that drew the Son of God from heaven. It is heart that will draw men to heaven. Men of heart is what the world needs to sympathize with its woe, to kiss away its sorrows, to compassionate its misery, and to alleviate its pain. Christ was eminently the man of sorrows, because he was preeminently the man of heart.

"Give me thy heart," is God's requisition of men. "Give me thy heart!Ý is man's demand of man.

A professional ministry is a heartless ministry. When salary plays a great part in the ministry, the heart plays little part. We may make preaching our business, and not put our hearts in the business. He who puts self to the front in his preaching puts heart to the rear. He who does not sow with his heart in his study will never reap a harvest for God. The closet is the heart's study. We will learn more about how to preach and what to preach there than we can learn in our libraries. "Jesus wept" is the shortest and biggest verse in the Bible. It is he who goes forth *weeping* (not preaching great sermons), bearing precious seed, who shall come again rejoicing, bringing his sheaves with him.

Praying gives sense, brings wisdom, broadens and strengthens the mind. The closet is a perfect school-teacher and schoolhouse for the preacher. Thought is not only brightened and clarified in prayer, but thought is born in prayer. We can learn more in an hour praying, when praying indeed, than from many hours in the study. Books are in the closet which can be found and read nowhere else. Revelations are made in the closet which are made nowhere else.

Chapter 14

Unction a Necessity

ALEXANDER KNOX, a Christian philosopher of the days of Wesley, not an adherent but a strong personal friend of Wesley, and with much spiritual sympathy with the Wesleyan movement, writes: "It is strange and lamentable, but I verily believe the fact to be that except among Methodists and Methodistical clergyman, there is not much interesting preaching in England. The clergy, too generally have absolutely lost the art. There is, I conceive, in the great laws of the moral world a kind of secret understanding like the affinities in chemistry, between rightly promulgated religious truth and the deepest feelings of the human mind. Where the one is duly exhibited, the other will respond. Did not our hearts burn within us?—but to this devout feeling is indispensable in the speaker. Now, I am obliged to state from my own observation that this *onction*, as the French not unfitly term it, is beyond all comparison more likely to be found in England in a Methodist conventicle than in a parish Church. This, and this alone, seems really to be that which fills the Methodist houses and thins the Churches. I am, I verily think, no enthusiast; I am a most sincere and cordial churchman, a humble disciple of the School of Hale and Boyle, of Burnet and Leighton. Now I must aver that when I was in this country, two years ago, I did not hear a single preacher who taught me like my own great masters but such as are deemed Methodistical. And I now despair of getting an atom of heart instruction from any other quarter. The Methodist preachers (however I may not always approve of all their expressions) do most assuredly diffuse this true religion and undefiled. I felt real pleasure last Sunday. I can bear witness that the preacher did at once speak the words of truth and soberness. There was no eloquence—the honest man never dreamed of such a thing'but there was far better: a cordial communication of vitalized truth. I say vitalized because what he declared to others it was impossible not to feel he lived on himself."

This unction is the art of preaching. The

preacher who never had this unction never had the art of preaching. The preacher who has lost this unction has lost the art of preaching. Whatever other arts he may have and retain?the art of sermon-making, the art of eloquence, the art of great, clear thinking, the art of pleasing an audience?he has lost the divine art of preaching. This unction makes God's truth powerful and interesting, draws and attracts, edifies, convicts, saves.

This unction vitalizes God's revealed truth, makes it living and life-giving. Even God's truth spoken without this unction is light, dead, and deadening. Though abounding in truth, though weighty with thought, though sparkling with rhetoric, though pointed by logic, though powerful by earnestness, without this divine unction it issues in death and not in life. Mr. Spurgeon says: "I wonder how long we might beat our brains before we could plainly put into word what is meant by preaching with unction. Yet he who preaches knows its presence, and he who hears soon detects its absence. Samaria, in famine, typifies a discourse without it. Jerusalem, with her feast of fat things, full of marrow, may represent a sermon enriched with it. Every one knows what the freshness of the morning is when orient pearls abound on every blade of grass, but who can describe it, much less produce it of itself? Such is the mystery of spiritual anointing. We know, but we cannot tell to others what it is. It is as easy as it is foolish, to counterfeit it. Unction is a thing which you cannot manufacture, and its counterfeits are worse than worthless. Yet it is, in itself, priceless, and beyond measure needful if you would edify believers and bring sinners to Christ."

Chapter 15

Unction, the Mark of True Gospel Preaching

U NCTION is that indefinable, indescribable something which an old, renowned Scotch preacher describes thus: "There is sometimes somewhat in preaching that cannot be ascribed either to matter or expression, and cannot be described what it is, or from whence it cometh, but with a sweet violence it pierceth into the heart and affections and comes immediately from the Word; but if there be any way to obtain such a thing, it is by the heavenly disposition of the speaker."

We call it unction. It is this unction which makes the word of God "quick and powerful, and sharper than any two-edged sword, piercing even to the dividing asunder of soul and spirit, and of the joints and marrow, and a discerner of the thoughts and intents of the heart." It is this unction which gives the words of the preacher such point, sharpness, and power, and which creates such friction and stir in many a dead congregation. The same truths have been told in the strictness of the letter, smooth as human oil could make them; but no signs of life, not a pulse throb; all as peaceful as the grave and as dead. The same preacher in the meanwhile receives a baptism of this unction, the divine inflatus is on him, the letter of the Word has been embellished and fired by this mysterious power, and the throbbings of life begin—life which receives or life which resists. The unction pervades and convicts the conscience and breaks the heart.

This divine unction is the feature which separates and distinguishes true gospel preaching from all other methods of presenting the truth, and which creates a wide spiritual chasm between the preacher who has it and the one who has it not. It backs and impregns revealed truth with all the energy of God. Unction is simply putting God in his own word and on his own preachers. By mighty and great prayerfulness and by continual prayerfulness, it is all potential and personal to the preacher; it inspires and clarifies his intellect, gives insight and grasp and projecting power; it gives to the preacher heart power, which is greater than head power; and tenderness, purity, force flow from the heart by it. Enlargement, freedom, fullness of thought, directness and simplicity of utterance are the fruits of this unction.

Often earnestness is mistaken for this unction. He who has the divine unction will be earnest in the very spiritual nature of things, but there may be a vast deal of earnestness without the least mixture of unction.

Earnestness and unction look alike from some points of view. Earnestness may be readily and without detection substituted or mistaken for unction. It requires a spiritual eye and a spiritual taste to discriminate.

Earnestness may be sincere, serious, ardent, and persevering. It goes at a thing with good will, pursues it with perseverance, and urges it with ardor; puts force in it. But all these forces do not rise higher than the mere human. The *man* is in it—the whole man, with all that he has of will and heart, of brain and genius, of planning and working and talking. He has set himself to some purpose which has mastered him, and he pursues to master it. There may be none of God in it. There may be little of God in it, because there is so much of the man in it. He may present pleas in advocacy of his earnest purpose which please or touch and move or overwhelm with conviction of their importance; and in all this earnestness may move along earthly ways, being propelled by human forces only, its altar made by earthly hands and its fire kindled by earthly flames. It is said of a rather famous preacher of gifts, whose construction of Scripture was to his fancy or purpose, that he "grew very eloquent over his own exegesis." So men grow exceeding earnest over their own plans or movements. Earnestness may be selfishness simulated.

What of unction? It is the indefinable in preaching which makes it preaching. It is that which distinguishes and separates preaching from all mere human addresses. It is the divine in preaching. It makes the preaching sharp to those who need sharpness. It distills as the dew to those who need to he refreshed. It is well described as:

> "*a two-edged sword*
> *Of heavenly temper keen,*
> *And double were the wounds*
>   *it made*
> *Wherever it glanced between.*
> *'Twas death to silt; 'twas life*
> *To all who mourned for sin.*
> *It kindled and it silenced strife,*
> *Made war and peace within.*"

This unction comes to the preacher not in the study but in the closet. It is heaven's distillation in answer to prayer. It is the sweetest exhalation of the Holy Spirit. It impregnates, suffuses, softens, percolates, cuts, and soothes. It carries the Word like dynamite, like salt, like sugar; makes the Word a soother, an arranger, a revealer, a searcher; makes the hearer a culprit or a saint, makes him weep like a child and live like a giant; opens his heart and his purse as gently, yet as strongly as the spring opens the leaves. This unction is not the gift of genius. It is not found in the halls of learning. No eloquence can woo it. No industry can win it. No prelatical hands can confer it. It is the gift of God—the signet set to his own messengers. It is heaven's knighthood given to the chosen true and brave ones who have sought this anointed honor through many an hour of tearful, wrestling prayer.

Earnestness is good and impressive: genius is gifted and great. Thought kindles and inspires, but it takes a diviner endowment, a more powerful energy than earnestness or genius or thought to break the chains of sin, to win estranged and depraved hearts to God, to repair the breaches and restore the Church to her old ways of purity and power. Nothing but this holy unction can do this.

Chapter 16

Much Prayer the Price of Unction

IN the Christian system unction is the anointing of the Holy Ghost, separating unto God's work and qualifying for it. This unction is the one divine enablement by which the preacher accomplishes the peculiar and saving ends of preaching. Without this unction there are no true spiritual results accomplished; the results and forces in preaching do not rise above the results of unsanctified speech. Without unction the former is as potent as the pulpit.

This divine unction on the preacher generates through the Word of God the spiritual results that flow from the gospel; and without this unction, these results are not secured. Many pleasant impressions may be made, but these all fall far below the ends of gospel preaching. This unction may be simulated. There are many things that look like it, there are many results that resemble its effects; but they are foreign to its results and to its nature. The fervor or softness excited by a pathetic or emotional sermon may look like the movements of the divine unction, but they have no pungent, perpetrating heart-breaking force. No heart-healing balm is there in these surface, sympathetic, emotional movements; they are not radical, neither sin-searching nor sin-curing.

This divine unction is the one distinguishing feature that separates true gospel preaching from all other methods of presenting truth. It backs and interpenetrates the revealed truth with all the force of God. It illumines the Word and broadens and enrichens the intellect and empowers it to grasp and apprehend the Word. It qualifies the preacher's heart, and brings it to that condition of tenderness, of purity, of force and light that are necessary to secure the highest results. This unction gives to the preacher liberty and enlargement of thought and soul—a freedom, fullness, and directness of utterance that can be secured by no other process.

Without this unction on the preacher the gospel has no more power to propagate itself than any other system of truth. This is the seal of its divinity. Unction in the preacher puts God in the gospel. Without the unction, God is absent, and the gospel is left to the low and unsatisfactory forces that the ingenuity, interest, or talents of men can devise to enforce and project its doctrines.

It is in this element that the pulpit oftener fails than in any other element. Just at this all-important point it lapses. Learning it may have, brilliancy and eloquence may delight and charm, sensation or less offensive methods may bring the populace in crowds, mental power may impress and enforce truth with all its resources; but without this unction, each and all these will be but as the fretful assault of the waters on a Gibraltar. Spray and foam may cover and spangle; but the rocks are there still, unimpressed and unimpressible. The human heart can no more be swept of its hardness and sin by these human forces than these rocks can be swept away by the ocean's ceaseless flow.

This unction is the consecration force, and its presence the continuous test of that consecration. It is this divine anointing on the preacher that secures his consecration to God and his work. Other forces and motives may call him to the work, but this only is consecration. A separation to God's work by the power of the Holy Spirit is the only consecration recognized by God as legitimate.

The unction, the divine unction, this heavenly anointing, is what the pulpit needs and must have. This divine and heavenly oil put on it by the imposition of God's hand must soften and lubricate the whole man—heart, head, spirit—until it separates him with a mighty separation from all earthly, secular, worldly, selfish motives and aims, separating him to everything that is pure and Godlike.

It is the presence of this unction on the preacher that creates the stir and friction in many a congregation. The same truths have been told in the strictness of the letter, but no ruffle has been seen, no pain or pulsation felt. All is quiet as a graveyard. Another preacher comes, and this mysterious influence is on him; the letter of the Word has been fired by the Spirit, the throes of a mighty movement are felt, it is the unction that pervades and stirs the conscience and breaks the heart. Unctionless preaching makes everything hard, dry, acrid, dead.

This unction is not a memory or an era of the past only; it is a present, realized, conscious fact. It belongs to the experience of the man as well as to his preaching. It is that which transforms him into the image of his divine Master, as well as that by which he declares the truths of Christ with power. It is so much the power in the ministry as to make all else seem feeble and vain without it, and by its presence to atone for the absence of all other and feebler forces.

This unction is not an inalienable gift. It is a conditional gift, and its presence is perpetuated and increased by the same process by which it was at first secured; by unceasing prayer to God, by impassioned desires after God, by estimating it, by seeking it with tireless ardor, by deeming all else loss and failure without it.

How and whence comes this unction? Direct from God in answer to prayer. Praying hearts only are the hearts filled with this holy oil; praying lips only are anointed with this divine unction.

Prayer, much prayer, is the price of preaching unction; prayer, much prayer, is the one, sole condition of keeping this unction. Without unceasing prayer the unction never comes to the preacher. Without perseverance in prayer, the unction, like the manna overkept, breeds worms.

Chapter 17

Prayer Marks Spiritual Leadership

THE apostles knew the necessity and worth of prayer to their ministry. They knew that their high commission as apostles, instead of relieving them from the necessity of prayer, committed them to it by a more urgent need; so that they were exceedingly jealous else some other important work should exhaust their time and prevent their praying as they ought; so they appointed laymen to look after the delicate and engrossing duties of ministering to the poor, that they (the apostles) might, unhindered, "give themselves continually to prayer and to the ministry of the word." Prayer is put first, and their relation to prayer is put most strongly—"give themselves to it," making a business of it, surrendering themselves to praying, putting fervor, urgency, perseverance, and time in it.

How holy, apostolic men devoted themselves to this divine work of prayer! "Night and day praying exceedingly," says Paul. "We will give ourselves continually to prayer" is the consensus of apostolic devotement. How these New Testament preachers laid themselves out in prayer for God's people! How they put God in full force into their Churches by their praying! These holy apostles did not vainly fancy that they had met their high and solemn duties by delivering faithfully God's word, but their preaching was made to stick and tell by the ardor and insistence of their praying. Apostolic praying was as taxing, toilsome, and imperative as apostolic preaching. They prayed mightily day and night to bring their people to the highest regions of faith and holiness. They prayed mightier still to hold them to this high spiritual altitude. The preacher who has never learned in the school of Christ the high and divine art of intercession for his people will never learn the art of preaching, though homiletics be poured into him by the ton, and though he be the most gifted genius in sermon-making and sermon-delivery.

The prayers of apostolic, saintly leaders do much in making saints of those who are not apostles. If the Church leaders in after years had been as particular and fervent in praying for their people as the apostles were, the sad, dark times of worldliness and apostasy had not marred the history and eclipsed the glory and arrested the advance of the Church. Apostolic praying makes apostolic saints and keeps apostolic times of purity and power in the Church.

What loftiness of soul, what purity and elevation of motive, what unselfishness, what self-sacrifice, what exhaustive toil, what ardor of spirit, what divine tact are requisite to be an intercessor for men!

The preacher is to lay himself out in prayer for his people; not that they might be saved, simply, but that they be mightily saved. The apostles laid themselves out in prayer that their saints might be perfect; not that they should have a little relish for the things of God, but that they "might be filled with all the fullness of God." Paul did not rely on his apostolic preaching to secure this end, but "for this cause he bowed his knees to the Father of our Lord Jesus Christ." Paul's praying carried Paul's converts farther along the highway of sainthood than Paul's preaching did. Epaphras did as much or more by prayer for the Colossian saints than by his preaching. He labored fervently always in prayer for them that "they might stand perfect and complete in all the will of God."

Preachers are preeminently God's leaders. They are primarily responsible for the condition of the Church. They shape its character, give tone and direction to its life.

Much every way depends on these leaders. They shape the times and the institutions. The Church is divine, the treasure it incases is heavenly, but it bears the imprint of the human. The treasure is in earthen vessels, and it smacks of the vessel. The Church of God makes, or is made by, its leaders. Whether it makes them or is made by them, it will be what its leaders are; spiritual if they are so, secular if they are, conglomerate if its leaders are. Israel's kings gave character to Israel's piety. A Church rarely revolts against or rises above the religion of its leaders. Strongly spiritual leaders; men of holy might, at the lead, are tokens of God's favor; disaster and weakness follow the wake of feeble or worldly leaders. Israel had fallen low when God gave children to be their princes and babes to rule over them. No happy state is predicted by the prophets when children oppress God's Israel and women rule over them. Times of spiritual leadership are times of great spiritual prosperity to the Church.

Prayer is one of the eminent characteristics of strong spiritual leadership. Men of mighty prayer are men of might and mold things. Their power with God has the conquering tread.

How can a man preach who does not get his message fresh from God in the closet? How can he preach without having his faith quickened, his vision cleared, and his heart warmed by his closeting with God? Alas, for the pulpit lips which are untouched by this closet flame. Dry and unctionless they will ever be, and truths divine will never come with power from such lips. As far as the real interests of religion are concerned, a pulpit without a closet will always be a barren thing.

A preacher may preach in an official, entertaining, or learned way without prayer, but between this kind of preaching and sowing God's precious seed with holy hands and prayerful, weeping hearts there is an immeasurable distance.

A prayerless ministry is the undertaker for all God's truth and for God's Church. He may have the most costly casket and the most beautiful flowers, but it is a funeral, notwithstanding the charmful array. A prayerless Christian will never learn God's truth; a prayerless ministry will never be able to teach God's truth. Ages of millennial glory have been lost by a prayerless Church. The coming of our Lord has been postponed indefinitely by a prayerless Church. Hell has enlarged herself and filled her dire caves in the presence of the dead service of a prayerless Church.

The best, the greatest offering is an offering of prayer. If the preachers of the twentieth century will learn well the lesson of prayer, and use fully the power of prayer, the millennium will come to its noon ere the century closes. "Pray without ceasing" is the trumpet call to the preachers of the twentieth century. If the twentieth century will get their texts, their thoughts, their words, their sermons in their closets, the next century will find a new heaven and a new earth. The old sin-stained and sin-eclipsed heaven and earth will pass away under the power of a praying ministry.

Chapter 18

Preachers Need the Prayers of the People

SOMEHOW the practice of praying in particular for the preacher has fallen into disuse or become discounted. Occasionally have we heard the practice arraigned as a disparagement of the ministry, being a public declaration by those who do it of the inefficiency of the ministry. It offends the pride of learning and self-sufficiency, perhaps, and these ought to be offended and rebuked in a ministry that is so derelict as to allow them to exist.

Prayer, to the preacher, is not simply the duty of his profession, a privilege, but it is a necessity. Air is not more necessary to the lungs than prayer is to the preacher. It is absolutely necessary for the preacher to pray. It is an absolute necessity that the preacher be prayed for. These two propositions are wedded into a union which ought never to know any divorce: *the preacher must pray; the preacher must be prayed for*. It will take all the praying he can do, and all the praying he can get done, to meet the fearful responsibilities and gain the largest, truest success in his great work. The true preacher, next to the cultivation of the spirit and fact of prayer in himself, in their intensest form, covets with a great covetousness the prayers of God's people.

The holier a man is, the more does he estimate prayer; the clearer does he see that God gives himself to the praying ones, and that the measure of God's revelation to the soul is the measure of the soul's longing, importunate prayer for God. Salvation never finds its way to a prayerless heart. The Holy Spirit never abides in a prayerless spirit. Preaching never edifies a prayerless soul. Christ knows nothing of prayerless Christians. The gospel cannot be projected by a prayerless preacher. Gifts, talents, education, eloquence, God's call, cannot abate the demand of prayer, but only intensify the necessity for the preacher to pray and to be prayed for. The more the preacher's eyes are opened to the nature, responsibility, and difficulties in his work, the more will he see, and if he be a true preacher the more will he feel, the necessity of prayer; not only the increasing demand to pray himself, but to call on others to help him by their prayers.

Paul is an illustration of this. If any man could

project the gospel by dint of personal force, by brain power, by culture, by personal grace, by God's apostolic commission, God's extraordinary call, that man was Paul. That the preacher must be a man given to prayer, Paul is an eminent example. That the true apostolic preacher must have the prayers of other good people to give to his ministry its full quota of success, Paul is a preeminent example. He asks, he covets, he pleads in an impassioned way for the help of all God's saints. He knew that in the spiritual realm, as elsewhere, in union there is strength; that the concentration and aggregation of faith, desire, and prayer increased the volume of spiritual force until it became overwhelming and irresistible in its power. Units of prayer combined, like drops of water, make an ocean which defies resistance. So Paul, with his clear and full apprehension of spiritual dynamics, determined to make his ministry as impressive, as eternal, as irresistible as the ocean, by gathering all the scattered units of prayer and precipitating them on his ministry. May not the solution of Paul's preeminence in labors and results, and impress on the Church and the world, be found in this fact that he was able to center on himself and his ministry more of prayer than others? To his brethren at Rome he wrote: "Now I beseech you, brethren, for the Lord Jesus Christ's sake, and for the love of the Spirit, that ye strive together with me in prayers to God for me." To the

Ephesians he says: "Praying always with all prayer and supplication in the Spirit, and watching thereunto with all perseverance and supplication for all saints; and for me, that utterance may be given unto me, that I may open my mouth boldly, to make known the mystery of the gospel." To the Colossians he emphasizes: "Withal praying also for us, that God would open unto us a door of utterance, to speak the mystery of Christ, for which I am also in bonds: that I may make it manifest as I ought to speak." To the Thessalonians he says sharply, strongly: "Brethren, pray for us." Paul calls on the Corinthian Church to help him: "Ye also helping together by prayer for us." This was to be part of their work. They were to lay to the helping hand of prayer. He in an additional and closing charge to the Thessalonian Church about the importance and necessity of their prayers says: "Finally, brethren, pray for us, that the word of the Lord may have free course, and be glorified, even as it is with you: and that we may be delivered from unreasonable and wicked men." He impresses the Philippians that all his trials and opposition can be made subservient to the spread of the gospel by the efficiency of their prayers for him. Philemon was to prepare a lodging for him, for through Philemon's prayer Paul was to be his guest.

Paul's attitude on this question illustrates his humility and his deep insight into the spiritual forces which project the gospel. More than this, it teaches a lesson for all times, that if Paul was so dependent on the prayers of God's saints to give his ministry success, how much greater the necessity that the prayers of God's saints be centered on the ministry of to-day!

Paul did not feel that this urgent plea for prayer was to lower his dignity, lessen his influence, or depreciate his piety. What if it did? Let dignity go, let influence be destroyed, let his reputation be marred—he must have their prayers. Called, commissioned, chief of the Apostles as he was, all his equipment was imperfect without the prayers of his people. He wrote letters everywhere, urging them to pray for him. Do you pray for your preacher? Do you pray for him in secret? Public prayers are of little worth unless they are founded on or followed up by private praying. The praying ones are to the preacher as Aaron and Hur were to Moses. They hold up his hands and decide the issue that is so fiercely raging around them.

The plea and purpose of the apostles were to put the Church to praying. They did not ignore the grace of cheerful giving. They were not ignorant of the place which religious activity and work occupied in the spiritual life; but not one nor all of these, in apostolic estimate or urgency, could at all compare in necessity and importance with prayer. The most sacred and urgent pleas were used, the most fervid exhortations, the most comprehensive and arousing words were uttered to enforce the all-important obligation and necessity of prayer.

"Put the saints everywhere to praying" is the burden of the apostolic effort and the keynote of apostolic success. Jesus Christ had striven to do this in the days of his personal ministry. As he was moved by infinite compassion at the ripened fields of earth perishing for lack of laborers and pausing in his own praying—he tries to awaken the stupid sensibilities of his disciples to the duty of prayer as he charges them, "Pray ye the Lord of the harvest that he will send forth laborers into his harvest." "And he spake a parable unto them to this end, that men ought always to pray and not to faint."

Chapter 19

Deliberation Necessary to Largest Results from Prayer

OUR devotions are not measured by the clock, but time is of their essence. The ability to wait and stay and press belongs essentially to our intercourse with God. Hurry, everywhere unseeming and damaging, is so to an alarming extent in the great business of communion with God. Short devotions are the bane of deep piety. Calmness, grasp, strength, are never the companions of hurry. Short devotions deplete spiritual vigor, arrest spiritual progress, sap spiritual foundations, blight the root and bloom of spiritual life. They are the prolific source of backsliding, the sure indication of a superficial piety; they deceive, blight, rot the seed, and impoverish the soil.

It is true that Bible prayers in word and print are short, but the praying men of the Bible were with God through many a sweet and holy wrestling hour. They won by few words but long waiting. The prayers Moses records may be short, but Moses prayed to God with fastings and mighty cryings forty days and nights.

The statement of Elijah's praying may be condensed to a few brief paragraphs, but doubtless Elijah, who when "praying he prayed," spent many hours of fiery struggle and lofty intercourse with God before he could, with assured boldness, say to Ahab, "There shall not be dew nor rain these years, but according to my word." The verbal brief of Paul's prayers is short, but Paul "prayed night and day exceedingly." The "Lord's Prayer" is a divine epitome for infant lips, but the man Christ Jesus prayed many an all-night ere his work was done; and his all-night and long-sustained devotions gave to his work its finish and perfection, and to his character the fullness and glory of its divinity.

Spiritual work is taxing work, and men are loath to do it. Praying, true praying, costs an outlay of serious attention and of time, which flesh and blood do not relish. Few persons are made of such strong fiber that they will make a costly outlay when surface work will pass as well in the market. We can habituate ourselves to our beggarly praying until it looks well to us, at least it keeps up a decent form and quiets conscience—the deadliest of opiates! We can slight our praying, and not realize the peril till the foundations are gone. Hurried devotions make weak faith, feeble convictions, questionable piety. To be little with God is to be little for God. To cut short the praying makes the whole religious character short, scrimp, niggardly, and slovenly.

It takes good time for the full flow of God into the spirit. Short devotions cut the pipe of God's full flow. It takes time in the secret places to get the full revelation of God. Little time and hurry mar the picture.

Henry Martyn laments that "want of private devotional reading and shortness of prayer through incessant sermon-making had produced much strangeness between God and his soul." He judged that he had dedicated too much time to public ministrations and too little to private communion with God. He was much impressed to set apart times for fasting and to devote times for solemn prayer. Resulting from this he records: "Was assisted this morning to pray for two hours." Said William Wilberforce, the peer of kings: "I must secure more time for private devotions. I have been living far too public for me. The shortening of private devotions starves the soul; it grows lean and faint. I have been keeping too late hours." Of a failure in Parliament he says: "Let me record my grief and shame, and all, probably, from private devotions having been contracted, and so God let me stumble." More solitude and earlier hours was his remedy.

More time and early hours for prayer would act like magic to revive and invigorate many a decayed spiritual life. More time and early hours for prayer would be manifest in holy living. A holy life would not be so rare or so difficult a thing if our devotions were not so short and hurried. A Christly temper in its sweet and passionless fragrance would not be so alien and hopeless a heritage if our closet stay were lengthened and intensified. We live shabbily because we pray meanly. Plenty of time to feast in our closets will bring marrow and fatness to our lives. Our ability to stay with God in our closet measures our ability to stay with God out of the closet. Hasty closet visits are deceptive, defaulting. We are not only deluded by them, but we are losers by them in many ways and in many rich legacies. Tarrying in the closet instructs and wins. We are taught by it, and the greatest victories are often the results of great waiting—waiting till words and plans are exhausted, and silent and patient waiting gains the crown. Jesus Christ asks with an affronted emphasis, "Shall not God avenge his own elect which cry day and night unto him?"

To pray is the greatest thing we can do: and to do it well there must be calmness, time, and deliberation; otherwise it is degraded into the littlest and meanest of things. True praying has the largest results for good; and poor praying, the least. We cannot do too much of real praying; we cannot do too little of the sham. We must learn anew the worth of prayer, enter anew the school of prayer. There is nothing which it takes more time to learn. And if we would learn the wondrous art, we must not give a fragment here and there—"A little talk with Jesus," as the tiny saintlets sing—but we must demand and hold with iron grasp the best hours of the day for God and prayer, or there will be no praying worth the name.

This, however, is not a day of prayer. Few men there are who pray. Prayer is defamed by preacher and priest. In these days of hurry and bustle, of electricity and steam, men will not take time to pray. Preachers there are who "say prayers" as a part of their programme, on regular or state occasions; but who "stirs himself up to take hold upon God?" Who prays as Jacob prayed—till he is crowned as a prevailing, princely intercessor? Who prays as Elijah prayed—till all the locked-up forces of nature were unsealed and a famine-stricken land bloomed as the garden of God? Who prayed as Jesus Christ prayed as out upon the mountain he "continued all night in prayer to God?" The apostles "gave themselves to prayer"—the most difficult thing to get men or even the preachers to do. Laymen there are who will give their money—some of them in rich abundance—but they will not "give themselves" to prayer, without which their money is but a curse. There are plenty of preachers who will preach and deliver great and eloquent addresses on the need of revival and the spread of the kingdom of God, but not many there are who will do that without which all preaching and organizing are worse than vain—pray. It is out of date, almost a lost art, and the greatest benefactor this age could have is the man who will bring the preachers and the Church back to prayer.

Chapter 20

A Praying Pulpit Begets a Praying Pew

O NLY glimpses of the great importance of prayer could the apostles get before Pentecost. But the Spirit coming and filling on Pentecost elevated prayer to its vital and all-commanding position in the gospel of Christ. The call now of prayer to every saint is the Spirit's loudest and most exigent call. Sainthood's piety is made, refined, perfected, by prayer. The gospel moves with slow and timid pace when the saints are not at their prayers early and late and long.

Where are the Christly leaders who can teach the modern saints how to pray and put them at it? Do we know we are raising up a prayerless set of saints? Where are the apostolic leaders who can put God's people to praying? Let them come to the front and do the work, and it will be the greatest work which can be done. An increase of educational facilities and a great increase of money force will be the direst curse to religion if they are not sanctified by more and better praying than we are doing. More praying will not come as a matter of course. The campaign for the twentieth or thirtieth century fund will not help our praying but hinder if we are not careful. Nothing but a specific effort from a praying leadership will avail. The chief ones must lead in the apostolic effort to radicate the vital importance and *fact* of prayer in the heart and life of the Church. None but praying leaders can have praying followers. Praying apostles will beget praying saints. A praying pulpit will beget praying pews. We do greatly need some body who can set the saints to this business of praying. We are not a generation of praying saints. Non-praying saints are a beggarly gang of saints who have neither the ardor nor the beauty nor the power of saints. Who will restore this breach? The greatest will he be of reformers and apostles, who can set the Church to praying.

We put it as our most sober judgment that the great need of the Church in this and all ages is men of such commanding faith, of such unsullied holiness, of such marked spiritual vigor and consuming zeal, that their prayers, faith, lives, and ministry will be of such a radical and aggressive form as to work spiritual revolutions which will form eras in individual and Church life.

We do not mean men who get up sensational stirs by novel devices, nor those who attract by a pleasing entertainment; but men who can stir things, and work revolutions by the preaching of God's Word and by the power of the Holy Ghost, revolutions which change the whole current of things.

Natural ability and educational advantages do not figure as factors in this matter; but capacity for faith, the ability to pray, the power of thorough consecration, the ability of self-littleness, an absolute losing of one's self in God's glory, and an ever-present and insatiable yearning and seeking after all the fullness of God—men who can set the Church ablaze for God; not in a noisy, showy way, but with an intense and quiet heat that melts and moves everything for God.

God can work wonders if he can get a suitable man. Men can work wonders if they can get God to lead them. The full endowment of the spirit that turned the world upside down would be eminently useful in these latter days. Men who can stir things mightily for God, whose spiritual revolutions change the whole aspect of things, are the universal need of the Church.

The Church has never been without these men; they adorn its history; they are the standing miracles of the divinity of the Church; their example and history are an unfailing inspiration and blessing. An increase in their number and power should be our prayer.

That which has been done in spiritual matters can be done again, and be better done. This was Christ's view. He said "Verily, verily, I say unto you, He that believeth on me, the works that I do shall he do also; and greater works than these shall he do; because I go unto my Father." The past has not exhausted the possibilities nor the demands for doing great things for God. The Church that is dependent on its past history for its miracles of power and grace is a fallen Church.

God wants elect men—men out of whom self and the world have gone by a severe crucifixion, by a bankruptcy which has so totally ruined self and the world that there is neither hope nor desire of recovery; men who by this insolvency and crucifixion have turned toward God perfect hearts.

Let us pray ardently that God's promise to prayer may be more than realized.

The Essentials of
Prayer

— 1925 —

Chapter 1

PRAYER TAKES IN THE WHOLE MAN

Prayer has to do with the entire man. Prayer takes in man in his whole being, mind, soul and body. It takes the whole man to pray, and prayer affects the entire man in its gracious results. As the whole nature of man enters into prayer, so also all that belongs to man is the beneficiary of prayer. All of man receives benefits in prayer. The whole man must be given to God in praying. The largest results in praying come to him who gives himself, all of himself, all that belongs to himself, to God. This is the secret of full consecration, and this is a condition of successful praying, and the sort of praying which brings the largest fruits.

The men of olden times who wrought well in prayer, who brought the largest things to pass, who moved God to do great things, were those who were entirely given over to God in their praying. God wants, and must have, all that there is in man in answering his prayers. He must have whole-hearted men through whom to work out His purposes and plans concerning men. God must have men in their entirety. No double-minded man need apply. No vacillating man can be used. No man with a divided allegiance to God, and the world and self, can do the praying that is needed.

Holiness is wholeness, and so God wants holy men, men whole-hearted and true, for his service and for the work of praying. "And the very God of peace sanctify you wholly; and I pray God your whole spirit and soul and body be preserved blameless unto the coming of our Lord Jesus Christ." These are the sort of men God wants for leaders of the hosts of Israel, and these are the kind out of which the praying class is formed. Man is a trinity in one, and yet man is neither a trinity nor a dual creature when he prays, but a unit. Man is one in all the essentials and acts and attitudes of piety. Soul, spirit and body are to unite in all things pertaining to life and godliness.

The body, first of all, engages in prayer, since it assumes the praying attitude in prayer. Prostration of the body becomes us in praying as well as prostration of the soul. The attitude of the body counts much in prayer, although it is true that the heart may be haughty and lifted up, and the mind listless and wandering, and the praying a mere form, even while the knees are bent in prayer.

Daniel kneeled three times a day in prayer. Solomon kneeled in prayer at the dedication of the temple. Our Lord in Gethsemane prostrated himself in that memorable season of praying just before his betrayal. Where there is earnest and faithful praying the body always takes on the form most suited to the state of the soul at the time. The body, that far, joins the soul in praying.

The entire man must pray. The whole man, life, heart, temper, mind, are in it. Each and all join in the prayer exercise. Doubt, double-mindedness, division of the affections, are all foreign to the closet. Character and conduct, undefiled, made whiter than snow, are mighty potencies, and are the most seemly beauties for the closet hour, and for the struggles of prayer.

A loyal intellect must conspire and add the energy and fire of its undoubting and undivided faith to that kind of an hour, the hour of prayer. Necessarily the mind enters into the praying. First of all, it takes thought to pray. The intellect teaches us we ought to pray. By serious thinking beforehand the mind prepares itself for approaching a throne of grace. Thought goes before entrance into the closet and prepares the way for true praying. It considers what will be asked for in the closet hour. True praying does not leave to the inspiration of the hour what will be the requests of that hour. As praying is asking for something definite of God, so, beforehand, the thought arises—"What shall I ask for at this hour?" All vain and evil and frivolous thoughts are eliminated, and the mind is given over entirely to God, thinking of him, of what is needed, and what has been received in the past. By every token, prayer, in taking hold of the entire man, does not leave out the mind. The very first step in prayer is a mental one. The disciples took that first step when they said unto Jesus at one time, "Lord, teach us to pray." We must be taught through the intellect, and just in so far as the intellect is given up to God in prayer, will we be able to learn well and readily the lesson of prayer.

Paul spreads the nature of prayer over the whole man. It must be so. It takes the whole man to embrace in its god-like sympathies the entire race of man—the sorrows, the sins and the death of Adam's fallen race. It takes the whole man to run parallel with God's high and sublime will in saving mankind. It takes the whole man to stand with our Lord Jesus Christ as the one mediator between God and sinful man. This is the doctrine Paul teaches in his prayer-directory in the second chapter of his first epistle to Timothy.

Nowhere does it appear so clearly that it requires the entire man in all departments of his being, to pray than in this teaching of Paul. It takes the whole man to pray till all the storms which agitate his soul are calmed to a great calm, till the stormy winds and waves cease as by a Godlike spell. It takes the whole man to pray till cruel tyrants and unjust rulers are changed in their natures and lives, as well as in their governing qualities, or till they cease to rule. It requires the entire man in praying till high and proud and unspiritual ecclesiastics become gentle, lowly and religious, till godliness and gravity bear rule in church and in state, in home and in business, in public as well as in private life.

It is man's business to pray; and it takes manly men to do it. It is godly business to pray and it takes godly men to do it. And it is godly men who give over themselves entirely to prayer. Prayer is far-reaching in its influence and in its gracious effects. It is intense and profound business which deals with God and His plans and purposes, and it takes whole-hearted men to do it. No half-hearted, half-brained, half-spirited effort will do for this serious, all-important, heavenly business. The whole heart, the whole brain, the whole spirit, must be in the matter of praying, which is so mightily to affect the characters and destinies of men. The answer of Jesus to the scribe as to what was the first and greatest commandment was as follows:

The Lord our God is one Lord; And thou shalt love the Lord thy God with all thy heart, and with thy soul, and with all thy mind, and with all thy strength.

In one word, the entire man without reservation must love God. So it takes the same entire man to do the praying which God requires of men. All the powers of man must be engaged in it. God cannot tolerate a divided heart in the love He requires of men, neither can He bear with a divided man in praying.

In the one hundred and nineteenth Psalm the Psalmist teaches this very truth in these words:

Blessed are they that keep his testimonies, and that seek him with the whole heart.

It takes whole-hearted men to keep God's commandments and it demands the same sort of men to seek God. These are they who are counted "blessed." Upon these whole-hearted ones God's approval rests.

Bringing the case closer home to himself the psalmist makes this declaration as to his practice: "With my whole heart have I sought thee; O let me not wander from thy commandments."

And further on, giving us his prayer for a wise and understanding heart, he tells us his purposes concerning the keeping of God's law:

Give me understanding and I shall keep thy law; Yea, I shall observe it with my whole heart.

Just as it requires a whole heart given to God to

gladly and fully obey God's commandments, so it takes a whole heart to do effectual praying.

Because it requires the whole man to pray, praying is no easy task. Praying is far more than simply bending the knee and saying a few words by rote.

> 'Tis not enough to bend the knee,
> And words of prayer to say;
> The heart must with the lips agree,
> Or else we do not pray.

Praying is no light and trifling exercise. While children should be taught early to pray, praying is no child's task. Prayer draws upon the whole nature of man. Prayer engages all the powers of man's moral and spiritual nature. It is this which explains somewhat the praying of our Lord described as in Hebrews 5:7:

Who in the days of his flesh, when he had offered up prayers and supplications, with strong crying and tears, unto him that was able to save him from death, and was heard in that he feared.

It takes only a moment's thought to see how such praying of our Lord drew mightily upon all the powers of his being, and called into exercise every part of his nature. This is the praying which brings the soul close to God and which brings God down to earth.

Body, soul and spirit are taxed and brought under tribute to prayer. David Brainerd makes this record of his praying:

God enabled me to agonise in prayer till I was wet with perspiration, though in the shade and in a cool place.

The Son of God in Gethsemane was in an agony of prayer, which engaged His whole being:

And when he was at the place, he said unto them, Pray ye that ye enter not into temptation. And he was withdrawn from them about a stone's cast, and kneeled down and prayed, saying, Father, if thou be willing, remove this cup from me; nevertheless, not my will, but thine, be done. And there appeared an angel unto him, from heaven, strengthening him. And being in an agony, he prayed more earnestly: and his sweat was as it were great drops of blood falling down to the ground. Luke 22:40-44.

Here was praying which laid its hands on every part of our Lord's nature, which called forth all the powers of his soul, his mind and his body. This was praying which took in the entire man.

Paul was acquainted with this kind of praying. In writing to the Roman Christians, he urges them to pray with him after this fashion:

Now I beseech you, brethren, for the Lord Jesus Christ's sake, and for the love of the Spirit, that ye strive together with me in your prayers to God for me.

The words, "strive together with me," tells of Paul's praying, and how much he put into it. It is not a docile request, not a little thing, this sort of praying, this "striving with me." It is of the nature of a great battle, a conflict to win, a great battle to be fought. The praying Christian, as the soldier, fights a life-and-death struggle. His honour, his immortality, and eternal life are all in it. This is praying as the athlete struggles for the mastery, and for the crown, and as he wrestles or runs a race. Everything depends on the strength he puts in it. Energy, ardour, swiftness, every power of his nature is in it. Every power is quickened and strained to its very utmost. Littleness, half-heartedness, weakness and laziness are all absent.

Just as it takes the whole man to pray successfully, so in turn the whole man receives the benefits of such praying. As every part of man's complex being enters into true praying, so every part of that same nature receives blessings from God in answer to such praying. This kind of praying engages our undivided hearts, our full consent to be the Lord's, our whole desires.

God sees to it that when the whole man prays, in turn the whole man shall be blessed. His body takes in the good of praying, for much praying is done specifically for the body. Food and raiment, health and bodily vigour, come in answer to praying. Clear mental action, right thinking, an enlightened understanding, and safe reasoning powers, come from praying. Divine guidance means God so moving and impressing the mind, that we shall make wise and safe decisions. "The meek will he guide in judgment."

Many a praying preacher has been greatly helped just at this point. The unction of the Holy One which comes upon the preacher invigorates the mind, loosens up thought and gives utterance. This is the explanation of former days when men of very limited education had such wonderful liberty of the Spirit in praying and in preaching. Their thoughts flowed as a stream of water. Their entire intellectual machinery felt the impulse of the divine Spirit's gracious influences.

And, of course, the soul receives large benefits in this sort of praying. Thousands can testify to this statement. So we repeat, that as the entire man comes into play in true, earnest effectual praying, so the entire man, soul, mind and body, receives the benefits of prayer.

Chapter 2

PRAYER AND HUMILITY

To be humble is to have a low estimate of one's self. It is to be modest, lowly, with a disposition to seek obscurity. Humility retires itself from the public gaze. It does not seek publicity nor hunt for high places, neither does it care for prominence. Humility is retiring in its nature. Self-abasement belongs to humility. It is given to self-depreciation. It never exalts itself in the eyes of others nor even in the eyes of itself. Modesty is one of its most prominent characteristics.

In humility there is the total absence of pride, and it is at the very farthest distance from anything like self-conceit. There is no self-praise in humility. Rather it has the disposition to praise others. "In honour preferring one another." It is not given to self-exaltation. Humility does not love the uppermost seats and aspire to the high places. It is willing to take the lowliest seat and prefers those places where it will be unnoticed. The prayer of humility is after this fashion:

> Never let the world break in,
> Fix a mighty gulf between;
> Keep me humble and unknown,
> Prized and loved by God alone.

Humility does not have its eyes on self, but rather on God and others. It is poor in spirit, meek in behaviour, lowly in heart. "With all lowliness and meekness, with long-suffering, forbearing one another in love."

The parable of the Pharisee and publican is a sermon in brief on humility and self-praise. The Pharisee, given over to self-conceit, wrapped up in himself, seeing only his own self-righteous deeds, catalogues his virtues before God, despising the poor publican who stands afar off. He exalts himself, gives himself over to self-praise, is self-centered, and goes away unjustified, condemned and rejected by God.

The publican sees no good in himself, is overwhelmed with self-depreciation, far removed from anything which would take any credit for any good in himself, does not presume to lift his eyes to heaven, but with downcast countenance smites himself on his breast, and cries out, "God be merciful to me, a sinner."

Our Lord with great preciseness gives us the sequel of the story of these two men, one utterly devoid of humility, the other utterly submerged in the spirit of self-depreciation and lowliness of mind.

I tell you this man went down to his house justified rather than the other; for every one that exalteth himself shall be abased; and he that humbleth himself shall be exalted. Luke 18:14.

God puts a great price on humility of heart. It is good to be clothed with humility as with a garment. It is written, "God resisteth the proud, but giveth grace to the humble." That which brings the praying soul near to God is humility of heart. That which gives wings to prayer is lowliness of mind. That which gives ready access to the throne of grace is self-depreciation. Pride, self-esteem, and self-praise effectually shut the door of prayer. He who would come to God must approach Him with self hid from his own eyes. He must not be puffed-up with self-conceit, nor be possessed with an over-estimate of his virtues and good works.

Humility is a rare Christian grace, of great price in the courts of heaven, entering into and being an inseparable condition of effectual praying. It gives access to God when other qualities fail. It takes many descriptions to describe it, and many definitions to define it. It is a rare and retiring grace. Its full portrait is found only in the Lord Jesus Christ. Our prayers must be set low before they can ever rise high. Our prayers must have much of the dust on them before they can ever have much of the glory of the skies in them. In our Lord's teaching, humility has such prominence in his system of religion, and is such a distinguishing feature of his character, that to leave it out of his lesson on prayer would be very unseemly, would not comport with his character, and would not fit into his religious system.

The parable of the Pharisee and publican stands out in such bold relief that we must again refer to it. The Pharisee seemed to be inured to prayer. Certainly he should have known by that time how to pray, but alas! like many others, he seemed never to have learned this invaluable lesson. He leaves business and business hours and walks with steady and fixed steps up to the house of prayer. The position and place are well-chosen by him. There is the sacred place, the sacred hour, and the sacred name, each and all invoked by this seemingly praying man. But this praying ecclesiastic, though schooled to prayer, by training and by habit, prays not. Words are uttered by him, but words are not prayer. God hears his words only to condemn him. A death-chill has come from those formal lips of prayer—a death-curse from God is on his words of prayer. A solution of pride has entirely poisoned the prayer offering of that hour. His entire praying has been impregnated with self-praise, self-congratulation, and self-exaltation. That season of temple going has had no worship whatever in it.

On the other hand, the publican, smitten with a deep sense of his sins and his inward sinfulness, realising how poor in spirit he is, how utterly devoid of anything like righteousness, goodness, or any quality which would commend him to God, his pride within utterly blasted and dead, falls down with humiliation and despair before God, while he utters a sharp cry for mercy for his sins and his guilt. A sense of sin and a realization of utter unworthiness has fixed the roots of humility deep down in his soul, and has oppressed self and eye and heart, downward to the dust. This is the picture of humility against pride in praying. Here we see by sharp contrast the utter worthlessness of self-righteousness, self-exaltation, and self-praise in praying, and the great value, the beauty and the divine commendation which comes to humility of heart, self-depreciation, and self-condemnation when a soul comes before God in prayer.

Happy are they who have no righteousness of their own to plead and no goodness of their own of which to boast. Humility flourishes in the soil of a true and deep sense of our sinfulness and our nothingness. Nowhere does humility grow so rankly and so rapidly and shine so brilliantly, as when it feels all guilty, confesses all sin, and trusts all grace. "I the chief of sinners am, but Jesus died for me." That is praying ground, the ground of humility, low down, far away seemingly, but in reality brought nigh by the blood of the Lord Jesus Christ. God dwells in the lowly places. He makes such lowly places really the high places to the praying soul.

> Let the world their virtue boast,
> Their works of righteousness;
> I, a wretch undone and lost,
> Am freely saved by grace;
> Other tide I disclaim,
> This, only this, is all my plea,
> I the chief of sinners am,
> But Jesus died for me.

Humility is an indispensable requisite of true prayer. It must be an attribute, a characteristic of prayer. Humility must be in the praying character as light is in the sun. Prayer has no beginning, no ending, no being, without humility. As a ship is made for the sea, so prayer is made for humility, and so humility is made for prayer.

Humility is not abstraction from self, nor does it ignore thought about self. It is a many-phased principle. Humility is born by looking at God, and his holiness, and then looking at self and man's unholiness. Humility loves obscurity and silence, dreads applause, esteems the virtues of others, excuses their faults with mildness, easily pardons injuries, fears contempt less and less, and sees baseness and falsehood in pride. A true nobleness and greatness are in humility. It knows and reveres the inestimable riches of the cross, and the humiliations of Jesus Christ. It fears the lustre of those virtues admired by men, and loves those that are more secret and which are prized by God. It draws comfort even from its own defects, through the abasement which they occasion. It prefers any degree of compunction before all light in the world.

Somewhat after this order of description is that definable grace of humility, so perfectly drawn in the publican's prayer, and so entirely absent from the prayer of the Pharisee. It takes many sittings to make a good picture of it.

Humility holds in its keeping the very life of prayer. Neither pride nor vanity can pray. Humility, though, is much more than the absence of vanity and pride. It is a positive quality, a substantial force, which energizes prayer. There is no power in prayer to ascend without it. Humility springs from a lowly estimate of ourselves and of our deservings. The Pharisee prayed not, though well schooled and accustomed to pray, because there was no humility in his praying. The publican prayed, though banned by the public and receiving no encouragement from church sentiment, because he prayed in humility.

To be clothed with humility is to be clothed with a praying garment. Humility is just feeling little because we are little. Humility is realising our unworthiness because we are unworthy, the feeling and declaring ourselves sinners because we are sinners. Kneeling well becomes us as the attitude of prayer, because it betokens humility.

The Pharisee's proud estimate of himself and his supreme contempt for his neighbour closed the gates of prayer to him, while humility opened wide those gates to the defamed and reviled publican.

That fearful saying of our Lord about the works of big, religious workers in the latter part of the Sermon on the Mount, is called out by proud estimates of work and wrong estimates of prayer:

Many shall say unto me in that day, Lord, Lord, have we not prophesied in thy name? and in thy name cast out devils? and in thy name done many wonderful works? And then will I profess unto them, I never knew you: depart from me, ye that work iniquity.

Humility is the first and last attribute of Christlike religion, and the first and last attribute of Christlikey praying. There is no Christ without humility. There is no praying without humility. If you would learn well the art of praying, then learn well the lesson of humility.

How graceful and imperative does the attitude of humility become to us! Humility is one of the unchanging and exacting attitudes of prayer. Dust, ashes, earth upon the head, sackcloth for the body, and fasting for the appetites, were the symbols of humility for the Old Testament saints. Sackcloth, fasting and ashes brought Daniel a lowliness before God, and brought Gabriel to him. The angels are fond of the sackcloth-and-ashes men.

How lowly the attitude of Abraham, the friend of God, when pleading for God to stay His wrath against Sodom! "Which am but sackcloth and ashes." With what humility does Solomon appear before God! His grandeur is abased, and his glory and majesty are retired as he assumes the rightful attitude before God: "I am but a little child, and know not how to go out or to come in."

The pride of doing sends its poison all through our praying. The same pride of being infects all our prayers, no matter how well-worded they may be. It was this lack of humility, this self-applauding, this self-exaltation, which kept the most religious man of Christ's day from being accepted of God. And the same thing will keep us in this day from being accepted of Him.

> O that now I might decrease!
> O that all I am might cease!
> Let me into nothing fall!
> Let my Lord be all in all.

Chapter 3

PRAYER AND DEVOTION

Devotion has a religious signification. The root of devotion is to devote to a sacred use. So that devotion in its true sense has to do with religious worship. It stands intimately connected with true prayer. Devotion is the particular frame of mind found in one entirely devoted to God. It is the spirit of reverence, of awe, of godly fear. It is a state of heart which appears before God in prayer and worship. It is foreign to everything like lightness of spirit, and is opposed to levity and noise and bluster. Devotion dwells in the realm of quietness and is still before God. It is serious, thoughtful, meditative.

Devotion belongs to the inner life and lives in the closet, but also appears in the public services of the sanctuary. It is a part of the very spirit of true worship, and is of the nature of the spirit of prayer.

Devotion belongs to the devout man, whose thoughts and feelings are devoted to God. Such a man has a mind given up wholly to religion, and possesses a strong affection for God and an ardent love for His house. Cornelius was "a devout man, one that feared God with all his house, which gave much alms to the people, and prayed always." "Devout men carried Stephen to his burial." "One Ananias, a devout man, according to the law," was sent unto Saul when he was blind, to tell him what the Lord would have him do. God can wonderfully use such men, for devout men are His chosen agents in carrying forward His plans.

Prayer promotes the spirit of devotion, while devotion is favourable to the best praying. Devotion furthers prayer and helps to drive prayer home to the object which it seeks. Prayer thrives in the atmosphere of true devotion. It is easy to pray when in the spirit of devotion. The attitude of mind and the state of heart implied in devotion make prayer effectual in reaching the throne of grace. God dwells where the spirit of devotion resides. All the graces of the Spirit are nourished and grow well in the environment created by devotion. Indeed, these graces grow nowhere else but here. The absence of a devotional spirit means death to the graces born in a renewed heart. True worship finds congeniality in the atmosphere made by a spirit of devotion. While prayer is helpful to devotion, at the same time devotion reacts on prayer, and helps us to pray.

Devotion engages the heart in prayer. It is not an easy task for the lips to try to pray while the heart is absent from it. The charge which God at one time made against His ancient Israel was, that they honoured Him with their lips while their hearts were far from Him.

The very essence of prayer is the spirit of devotion. Without devotion prayer is an empty form, a vain round of words. Sad to say, much of this kind of prayer prevails, today, in the Church. This is a busy age, bustling and active, and this bustling spirit has invaded the Church of God. Its religious performances are many. The Church works at religion with the order, precision and force of real machinery. But too often it works with the heartlessness of the machine. There is much of the treadmill movement in our ceaseless round and routine of religious doings. We pray without praying. We sing without singing with the Spirit and the understanding. We have music without the praise of God being in it, or near it. We go to Church by habit, and come home all too gladly when the benediction is pronounced. We read our accustomed chapter in the Bible, and feel quite relieved when the task is done. We say our prayers by rote, as a schoolboy recites his lesson, and are not sorry when the Amen is uttered.

Religion has to do with everything but our hearts. It engages our hands and feet, it takes hold of our voices, it lays its hands on our money, it affects even the postures of our bodies, but it does not take hold of our affections, our desires, our zeal, and make us serious, desperately in earnest, and cause us to be quiet and worshipful in the presence of God. Social affinities attract us to the house of God, not the spirit of the occasion. Church membership keeps us after a fashion decent in outward conduct and with some shadow of loyalty to our baptismal vows, but the heart is not in the thing. It remains cold, formal, and unimpressed amid all this outward performance, while we give ourselves over to self-congratulation that we are doing wonderfully well religiously.

Why all these sad defects in our piety? Why this modern perversion of the true nature of the religion of Jesus Christ? Why is the modern type of religion so much like a jewel-case, with the precious jewels gone? Why so much of this handling religion with the hands, often not too clean or unsoiled, and so little of it felt in the heart and witnessed in the life?

The great lack of modern religion is the spirit of devotion. We hear sermons in the same spirit with which we listen to a lecture or hear a speech. We visit the house of God just as if it were a common place, on a level with the theatre, the lecture-room or the forum. We look upon the minister of God not as the divinely-called man of God, but merely as a sort of public speaker, on a plane with the politician, the lawyer, or the average speech maker, or the lecturer. Oh, how the spirit of true and genuine devotion would radically change all this for the better! We handle sacred things just as if they were the things of the world. Even the sacrament of the Lord's Supper becomes a mere religious performance, no preparation for it before-hand, and no meditation and prayer afterward. Even the sacrament of Baptism has lost much of its solemnity, and degenerated into a mere form, with nothing specially in it.

We need the spirit of devotion, not only to salt our secularities, but to make praying real prayers. We need to put the spirit of devotion into Monday's business as well as in Sunday's worship. We need the spirit of devotion, to recollect always the presence of God, to be always doing the will of God, to direct all things always to the glory of God.

The spirit of devotion puts God in all things. It puts God not merely in our praying and Church going, but in all the concerns of life. "Whether, therefore, ye eat or drink, or whatsoever ye do, do all to the glory of God." The spirit of devotion makes the common things of earth sacred, and the little things great. With this spirit of devotion, we go to business on Monday directed by the very same influence, and inspired by the same influences by which we went to Church on Sunday. The spirit of devotion makes a Sabbath out of Saturday, and transforms the shop and the office into a temple of God.

The spirit of devotion removes religion from being a thin veneer, and puts it into the very life and being of our souls. With it religion ceases to be doing a mere work, and becomes a heart, sending its rich blood through every artery and beating with the pulsations of vigourous and radiant life.

The spirit of devotion is not merely the aroma of religion, but the stalk and stem on which religion grows. It is the salt which penetrates and makes savoury all religious acts. It is the sugar which sweetens duty, self-denial and sacrifice. It is the bright colouring which relieves the dullness of religious performances. It dispels frivolity and drives away all skin-deep forms of worship, and makes worship a serious and deep-seated service, impregnating body, soul and spirit with its heavenly infusion. Let us ask in all seriousness, has this highest angel of heaven, this heavenly spirit of devotion, this brightest and best angel of earth, left us? When the angel of devotion has gone, the angel of prayer has lost its wings, and it becomes a deformed and loveless thing.

The ardour of devotion is in prayer. In Rev. 4:8, we read: "And they rest not day nor night, saying, Holy, Holy, Holy, Lord God Almighty, which was, and is, and is to come." The inspiration and centre of their rapturous devotion is the holiness of God. That holiness of God claims their attention, inflames their devotion. There is nothing cold, nothing dull, nothing wearisome about them or their heavenly worship. "They rest not day nor night." What zeal! What unfainting ardour and ceaseless rapture! The ministry of prayer, if it be anything worthy of the name, is a ministry of ardour, a ministry of unwearied and intense longing after God and after His holiness.

The spirit of devotion pervades the saints in heaven and characterizes the worship of heaven's angelic intelligences. No devotionless creatures are in that heavenly world God is there, and His very presence begets the spirit of reverence, of awe, and of filial fear. If we would be partakers with them after death, we must first learn the spirit of devotion on earth before we get there.

These living creatures in their restless, tireless, attitude after God, and their rapt devotion to His holiness, are the perfect symbols and illustrations of true prayer and its ardour. Prayer must be aflame. Its ardour must consume. Prayer without fervour is as a sun without light or heat, or as a flower without beauty or fragrance. A soul devoted to God is a fervent soul, and prayer is the creature of that flame. He only can truly pray who is all aglow for holiness, for God, and for heaven.

Activity is not strength. Work is not zeal. Moving about is not devotion. Activity often is the unrecognised symptom of spiritual weakness. It may be hurtful to piety when made the substitute for real devotion in worship. The colt is much more active than its mother, but she is the wheel-horse of the team, pulling the load without noise or bluster or show. The child is more active than the father, who may be bearing the rule and burdens of an empire on his heart and shoulders. Enthusiasm is more active than faith, though it cannot remove mountains nor call into action any of the omnipotent forces which faith can command.

A feeble, lively, showy religious activity may spring from many causes. There is much running around, much stirring about, much going here and there, in present-day Church life, but sad to say, the spirit of genuine, heartfelt devotion is strangely lacking. If there be real spiritual life, a deep-toned activity will spring from it. But it is an activity springing from strength and not from weakness. It is an activity which has deep roots, many and strong.

In the nature of things, religion must show much of its growth above ground. Much will be seen and be evident to the eye. The flower and fruit of a holy life, abounding in good works, must be seen. It cannot be otherwise. But the surface growth must be based on a vigourous growth of unseen life and hidden roots. Deep down in the renewed nature must the roots of religion go which is seen on the outside. The external must have a deep internal groundwork. There must be much of the invisible and the underground growth, or else the life will be feeble and short-lived and the external growth sickly and fruitless.

In the Book of the prophet Isaiah these words are written:

"They that wait on the Lord shall renew their strength; they shall mount up with wings as eagles; they shall run and not be weary; and they shall walk and not faint." Isaiah 40:31.

This is the genesis of the whole matter of activity and strength of the most energetic, exhaustless and untiring nature. All this is the result of waiting on God.

There may be much of activity induced by drill, created by enthusiasm, the product of the weakness of the flesh, the inspiration of volatile, short-lived forces. Activity is often at the expense of more solid, useful elements, and generally to the total neglect of prayer. To be too busy with God's work to commune with God, to be busy with doing Church work without taking time to talk to God about His work, is the highway to backsliding, and many people have walked therein to the hurt of their immortal souls.

Notwithstanding great activity, great enthusiasm, and much hurrah for the work, the work and the activity will be but blindness without the cultivation and the maturity of the graces of prayer.

Chapter 4

PRAYER, PRAISE AND THANKSGIVING

Prayer, praise and thanksgiving all go in company. A close relationship exists between them. Praise and thanksgiving are so near alike that it is not easy to distinguish between them or define them separately. The Scriptures join these three things together. Many are the causes for thanksgiving and praise. The Psalms are filled with many songs of praise and hymns of thanksgiving, all pointing back to the results of prayer. Thanksgiving includes gratitude. In fact thanksgiving is but the expression of an inward conscious gratitude to God for mercies received. Gratitude is an inward emotion of the soul, involuntarily arising therein, while thanksgiving is the voluntary expression of gratitude.

Thanksgiving is oral, positive, active. It is the

giving out of something to God. Thanksgiving comes out into the open. Gratitude is secret, silent, negative, passive, not showing its being till expressed in praise and thanksgiving. Gratitude is felt in the heart. Thanksgiving is the expression of that inward feeling.

Thanksgiving is just what the word itself signifies—the giving of thanks to God. It is giving something to God in words which we feel at heart for blessings received. Gratitude arises from a contemplation of the goodness of God. It is bred by serious meditation on what God has done for us. Both gratitude and thanksgiving point to, and have to do with God and His mercies. The heart is consciously grateful to God. The soul gives expression to that heartfelt gratitude to God in words or acts.

Gratitude is born of meditation on God's grace and mercy. "The Lord hath done great things for us, whereof we are glad." Herein we see the value of serious meditation. "My meditation of him shall be sweet." Praise is begotten by gratitude and a conscious obligation to God for mercies given. As we think of mercies past, the heart is inwardly moved to gratitude.

> "I love to think on mercies past,
> And future good implore;
> And all my cares and sorrows cast
> On Him whom I adore."

Love is the child of gratitude. Love grows as gratitude is felt, and then breaks out into praise and thanksgiving to God: "I love the Lord because he hath heard my voice and my supplication." Answered prayers cause gratitude, and gratitude brings forth a love that declares it will not cease praying: "Because he hath inclined his ear unto me, therefore will I call upon him as long as I live." Gratitude and love move to larger and increased praying.

Paul appeals to the Romans to dedicate themselves wholly to God, a living sacrifice, and the constraining motive is the mercies of God:

"I beseech you, therefore, brethren, by the mercies of God, that ye present your bodies a living sacrifice, holy, acceptable unto God, which is your reasonable service."

Consideration of God's mercies not only begets gratitude, but induces a large consecration to God of all we have and are. So that prayer, thanksgiving and consecration are all linked together inseparably.

Gratitude and thanksgiving always looks back at the past though it may also take in the present. But prayer always looks to the future. Thanksgiving deals with things already received. Prayer deals with things desired, asked for and expected. Prayer turns to gratitude and praise when the things asked for have been granted by God.

As prayer brings things to us which beget gratitude and thanksgiving, so praise and gratitude promote prayer, and induce more praying and better praying.

Gratitude and thanksgiving forever stand opposed to all murmurings at God's dealings with us, and all complainings at our lot. Gratitude and murmuring never abide in the same heart at the same time. An unappreciative spirit has no standing beside gratitude and praise. And true prayer corrects complaining and promotes gratitude and thanksgiving. Dissatisfaction at one's lot, and a disposition to be discontented with things which come to us in the providence of God, are foes to gratitude and enemies to thanksgiving.

The murmurers are ungrateful people. Appreciative men and women have neither the time nor disposition to stop and complain. The bane of the wilderness-journey of the Israelites on their way to Canaan was their proneness to murmur and complain against God and Moses. For this, God was several times greatly grieved, and it took the strong praying of Moses to avert God's wrath because of these murmurings. The absence of gratitude left no room nor disposition for praise and thanksgiving, just as it is so always. But when these same Israelites were brought through the Red Sea dry shod, while their enemies were destroyed, there was a song of praise led by Miriam, the sister of Moses. One of the leading sins of these Israelites was forgetfulness of God and His mercies, and ingratitude of soul. This brought forth murmurings and lack of praise, as it always does.

When Paul wrote to the Colossians to let the word of Christ dwell in their hearts richly and to let the peace of God rule therein, he said to them, "and be ye thankful," and adds, "admonishing yourselves in psalms and hymns and spiritual songs, singing with grace in your hearts unto the Lord."

Further on, in writing to these same Christians, he joins prayer and thanksgiving together: "Continue in prayer, and watch in the same with thanksgiving."

And writing to the Thessalonians, he again joins them in union: "Rejoice evermore. Pray without ceasing. In everything give thanks, for this is the will of God concerning you."

> "We thank Thee, Lord of heaven
> and earth,
> Who hast preserved us from our
> birth;
> Redeemed us oft from death and
> dread,
> And with Thy gifts our table
> spread."

Wherever there is true prayer, there thanksgiving and gratitude stand hard by, ready to respond to the answer when it comes. For as prayer brings the answer, so the answer brings forth gratitude and praise. As prayer sets God to work, so answered prayer sets thanksgiving to work. Thanksgiving follows answered prayer just as day succeeds night.

True prayer and gratitude lead to full consecration, and consecration leads to more praying and better praying. A consecrated life is both a prayer-life and a thanksgiving life.

The spirit of praise was once the boast of the primitive Church. This spirit abode on the tabernacles of these early Christians, as a cloud of glory out of which God shined and spoke. It filled their temples with the perfume of costly, flaming incense. That this spirit of praise is sadly deficient in our present-day congregations must be evident to every careful observer. That it is a mighty force in projecting the Gospel, and its body of vital forces, must be equally evident. To restore the spirit of praise to our congregations should be one of the main points with every true pastor. The normal state of the Church is set forth in the declaration made to God in Psalm 65: "Praise waiteth for thee, O Lord, and unto thee shall the vow be performed."

Praise is so distinctly and definitely wedded to prayer, so inseparably joined, that they cannot be divorced. Praise is dependent on prayer for its full volume and its sweetest melody.

Singing is one method of praise, not the highest

it is true, but it is the ordinary and usual form. The singing service in our churches has much to do with praise, for according to the character of the singing will be the genuineness or the measure of praise. The singing may be so directed as to have in it elements which deprave and debauch prayer. It may be so directed as to drive away everything like thanksgiving and praise. Much of modern singing in our churches is entirely foreign to anything like hearty, sincere praise to God.

The spirit of prayer and of true praise go hand in hand. Both are often entirely dissipated by the flippant, thoughtless, light singing in our congregations. Much of the singing lacks serious thought and is devoid of everything like a devotional spirit. Its lustiness and sparkle may not only dissipate all the essential features of worship, but may substitute the flesh for the spirit.

Giving thanks is the very life of prayer. It is its fragrance and music, its poetry and its crown. Prayer bringing the desired answer breaks out into praise and thanksgiving. So that whatever interferes with and injures the spirit of prayer necessarily hurts and dissipates the spirit of praise.

The heart must have in it the grace of prayer to sing the praise of God. Spiritual singing is not to be done by musical taste or talent, but by the grace of God in the heart. Nothing helps praise so mightily as a gracious revival of true religion in the Church.

The conscious presence of God inspires song. The angels and the glorified ones in heaven do not need artistic precentors to lead them, nor do they care for paid choirs to chime in with their heavenly doxologies of praise and worship. They are not dependent on singing schools to teach them the notes and scale of singing. Their singing involuntarily breaks forth from the heart.

God is immediately present in the heavenly assemblies of the angels and the spirits of just men made perfect. His glorious presence creates the song, teaches the singing, and impregnates their notes of praise. It is so on earth. God's presence begets singing and thanksgiving, while the absence of God from our congregations is the death of song, or, which amounts to the same, makes the singing lifeless, cold and formal. His conscious presence in our churches would bring back the days of praise and would restore the full chorus of song.

Where grace abounds, song abounds. When God is in the heart, heaven is present and melody is there, and the lips overflow out of the abundance of the heart. This is as true in the private life of the believer as it is so in the congregations of the saints. The decay of singing, the dying down and out of the spirit of praise in song, means the decline of grace in the heart and the absence of God's presence from the people.

The main design of all singing is for God's ear

and to attract His attention and to please Him. It is "to the Lord," for His glory, and to His honour. Certainly it is not for the glorification of the paid choir, to exalt the wonderful musical powers of the singers, nor is it to draw the people to the church, but it is for the glory of God and the good of the souls of the congregation. Alas! How far has the singing of choirs of churches of modern times departed from this idea! It is no surprise that there is no life, no power, no unction, no spirit, in much of the Church singing heard in this day. It is sacrilege for any but sanctified hearts and holy lips to direct the singing part of the service of God's house of prayer. Much of the singing in churches would do credit to the opera house, and might satisfy as mere entertainments, pleasing the ear, but as a part of real worship, having in it the spirit of praise and prayer, it is a fraud, an imposition on spiritually minded people, and entirely unacceptable to God. The cry should go out afresh, "Let all the people praise the Lord," for "it is good to sing praises unto our God; for it is pleasant; and praise is comely."

The music of praise, for there is real music of soul in praise, is too hopeful and happy to be denied. All these are in the "giving of thanks." In Philippians, prayer is called "requests." "Let your requests be made known unto God," which describes prayer as an asking for a gift, giving prominence to the thing asked for, making it emphatic, something to be given by God and received by us, and not something to be done by us. And all this is closely connected with gratitude to God, "with thanksgiving, let your requests be made known unto God."

God does much for us in answer to prayer, but we need from Him many gifts, and for them we are to make special prayer. According to our special needs, so must our praying be. We are to be special and particular and bring to the knowledge of God by prayer, supplication and thanksgiving, our particular requests, the things we need, the things we greatly desire. And with it all, accompanying all these requests, there must be thanksgiving.

It is indeed a pleasing thought that what we are called upon to do on earth, to praise and give thanks, the angels in heaven and the redeemed disembodied spirits of the saints are doing also. It is still further pleasing to contemplate the glorious hope that what God wants us to do on earth, we will be engaged in doing throughout an unending eternity. Praise and thanksgiving will be our blessed employment while we remain in heaven. Nor will we ever grow weary of this pleasing task.

Joseph Addison sets before us, in verse, this pleasing prospect:

> "Through every period of my life
> Thy goodness I'll pursue;

And after death, in distant worlds,
The pleasing theme renew.
"Through all eternity to Thee
A grateful song I'll raise;
But Oh! eternity's too short
To utter all Thy praise."

Chapter 5

PRAYER AND TROUBLE

Trouble and prayer are closely related to each other. Prayer is of great value to trouble. Trouble often drives men to God in prayer, while prayer is but the voice of men in trouble. There is great value in prayer in the time of trouble. Prayer often delivers out of trouble, and still oftener gives strength to bear trouble, ministers comfort in trouble, and begets patience in the midst of trouble. Wise is he in the day of trouble who knows his true source of strength and who fails not to pray.

Trouble belongs to the present state of man on earth. "Man that is born of a woman is of few days and full of trouble." Trouble is common to man. There is no exception in any age or clime or station. Rich and poor alike, the learned and the ignorant, one and all are partakers of this sad and painful inheritance of the fall of man. "There hath no temptation taken you but such as is common to man." The "day of trouble" dawns on every one at some time in his life. "The evil days come and the years draw nigh" when the heart feels its heavy pressure.

That is an entirely false view of life and shows supreme ignorance that expects nothing but sunshine and looks only for ease, pleasure and flowers. It is this class who are so sadly disappointed and surprised when trouble breaks into their lives. These are the ones who know not God, who know nothing of His disciplinary dealings with His people and who are prayerless.

What an infinite variety there is in the troubles of life! How diversified the experiences of men in the school of trouble! No two people have the same troubles under like environments. God deals with no two of His children in the same way. And as God varies His treatment of His children, so trouble is varied. God does not repeat Himself. He does not run in a rut. He has not one pattern for every child. Each trouble is proportioned to each child. Each one is dealt with according to his own peculiar case.

Trouble is God's servant, doing His will unless He is defeated in the execution of that will. Trouble is under the control of Almighty God, and is one of His most efficient agents in fulfilling His purposes and in perfecting His saints. God's hand is in every trouble which breaks into the lives of men. Not that He directly and arbitrarily orders every unpleasant experience of life. Not that He is personally responsible for every painful and afflicting thing which comes into the lives of His people. But no trouble is ever turned loose in this world and comes into the life of saint or sinner, but comes with Divine permission, and is allowed to exist and do its painful work with God's hand in it or on it, carrying out His gracious designs of redemption.

All things are under Divine control. Trouble is neither above God nor beyond His control. It is not something in life independent of God. No matter from what source it springs nor whence it arises, God is sufficiently wise and able to lay His hand upon it without assuming responsibility for its origin, and work it into His plans and purposes concerning the highest welfare of His saints. This is the explanation of that gracious statement in Romans, so often quoted, but the depth of whose meaning has rarely been sounded, "And we know that all things work together for good to them that love God."

Even the evils brought about by the forces of nature are His servants, carrying out His will and fulfilling His designs. God even claims the locusts, the cankerworm, the caterpillar are His servants,

"My great army," used by Him to correct His people and discipline them.

Trouble belongs to the disciplinary part of the moral government of God. This is a life of probation, where the human race is on probation. It is a season of trial. Trouble is not penal in its nature. It belongs to what the Scriptures call "chastening." "Whom the Lord loveth he chasteneth, and scourgeth every son whom he receiveth." Speaking accurately, punishment does not belong to this life. Punishment for sin will take place in the next world. God's dealings with people in this world are of the nature of discipline. They are corrective processes in His plans concerning man. It is because of this that prayer comes in when trouble arises. Prayer belongs to the discipline of life.

As trouble is not sinful in itself, neither is it the evidence of sin. Good and bad alike experience trouble. As the rain falls alike on the just and unjust, so drouth likewise comes to the righteous and the wicked. Trouble is no evidence whatever of the Divine displeasure. Scripture instances without number disprove any such idea. Job is a case in point, where God bore explicit testimony to his deep piety, and yet God permitted Satan to afflict him beyond any other man for wise and beneficent purposes. Trouble has no power in itself to interfere with the relations of a saint to God. "Who shall separate us from the love of Christ? Shall tribulation, or distress, or persecution, or famine, or nakedness, or peril, or sword?"

Three words practically the same in the processes of Divine discipline are found, temptation, trial and trouble, and yet there is a difference between them. Temptation is really a solicitation to evil arising from the devil or born in the carnal nature of man. Trial is testing. It is that which proves us, tests us, and makes us stronger and better when we submit to the trial and work together with God in it "My brethren, count it all joy when ye fall into divers temptations; knowing this, that the trying of your faith worketh patience."

Peter speaks along the same line:

"Wherein ye greatly rejoice, now for a season, if need be, ye are in heaviness through manifold temptations; that the trial of your faith being much more precious than that of gold that perisheth, though it be tried with fire, might be found unto praise, and honor and glory at the appearing of Jesus Christ."

The third word is trouble itself, which covers all the painful, sorrowing, and grievous events of life. And yet temptations and trials might really become troubles. So that all evil days in life might well be classed under the head of the "time of trouble." And such days of trouble are the lot of all men. Enough to know that trouble, no matter from what source it comes; becomes in God's hand His own agent to accomplish His gracious work concerning those who submit patiently to Him, who recognise Him in prayer, and who work together with God.

Let us settle down at once to the idea that trouble arises not by chance, and neither occurs by what men call accident. "Although affliction cometh not forth of the dust, neither doth trouble spring out of the ground, yet man is born unto trouble as the sparks fly upward." Trouble naturally belongs to God's moral government, and is one of His invaluable agents in governing the world.

When we realise this, we can the better understand much that is recorded in the Scriptures, and can have a clearer conception of God's dealings with His ancient Israel. In God's dealings with them, we find what is called a history of Divine Providence, and providence always embraces trouble. No one can understand the story of Joseph and his old father Jacob unless he takes into the account trouble and its varied offices. God takes account of trouble when He urges His prophet Isaiah on the wise:

"Comfort ye, comfort ye my people, saith your God. Speak ye comfortably to Jerusalem, and cry unto her that her warfare is accomplished, that her iniquity is pardoned."

There is a distinct note of comfort in the Gospel for the praying saints of the Lord, and He is a wise scribe in Divine things who knows how to minister this comfort to the broken-hearted and sad ones of earth. Jesus Himself said to His sad disciples, "I will not leave you comfortless."

All the foregoing has been said that we may rightly appreciate the relationship of prayer to trouble. In the time of trouble, where does prayer come in? The Psalmist tells us: "Call upon me in the day of trouble; I will deliver thee, and thou shalt glorify me." Prayer is the most appropriate thing for a soul to do in the "time of trouble." Prayer recognises God in the day of trouble. "It is the Lord; let him do what seemeth him good." Prayer sees God's hand in trouble, and prays about it. Nothing more truly shows us our helplessness than when trouble comes. It brings the strong man low, it discloses our weakness, it brings a sense of helplessness. Blessed is he who knows how to turn to God in "the time of trouble." If trouble is of the Lord, then the most natural thing to do is to carry the trouble to the Lord, and seek grace and patience and submission. It is the time to inquire in the trouble, "Lord, what wilt thou have me to do?" How natural and reasonable for the soul, oppressed, broken, and bruised, to bow low at the footstool of mercy and seek the face of God? Where could a soul in trouble more likely find solace than in the closet?

Alas! trouble does not always drive men to God in prayer. Sad is the case of him who, when trouble bends his spirit down and grieves his heart, yet knows not whence the trouble comes nor knows how to pray about it. Blessed is the man who is driven by trouble to his knees in prayer!

> "Trials must and will befall;
> But with humble faith to see
> Love inscribed upon them all—
> This is happiness to me.
> "Trials make the promise sweet,
> Trials give new life to prayer;
> Bring me to my Saviour's feet,
> Lay me low, and keep me there."

Prayer in the time of trouble brings comfort, help, hope, and blessings, which, while not removing the trouble, enable the saint the better to bear it and to submit to the will of God. Prayer opens the eyes to see God's hand in trouble. Prayer does not interpret God's providences, but it does justify them and recognise God in them. Prayer enables us to see wise ends in trouble. Prayer in trouble drives us away from unbelief, saves us from doubt, and delivers from all vain and foolish questionings because of our painful experiences. Let us not lose sight of the tribute paid to Job when all his troubles came to the culminating point: "In all this Job sinned not, nor charged God foolishly."

Alas! for vain, ignorant men, without faith in God and knowing nothing of God's disciplinary processes in dealing with men, who charge God foolishly when troubles come, and who are tempted to "curse God." How silly and vain are the complainings, the murmurings and the rebellion of men in the time of trouble! What need to read again the story of the Children of Israel in the wilderness! And how useless is all our fretting, our worrying over trouble, as if such unhappy doings on our part could change things! "And which of you with taking thought, can add to his stature one cubit?" How much wiser, how much better, how much easier to bear life's troubles when we take everything to God in prayer?

Trouble has wise ends for the praying ones, and these find it so. Happy is he who, like the Psalmist, finds that his troubles have been blessings in disguise. "It is good for me that I have been afflicted, that I might learn thy statutes. I know, O Lord, that thy judgments are right, and that thou in faithfulness hast afflicted me."

> "O who could bear life's stormy
> doom,
> Did not Thy wing of love
> Come brightly wafting through the
> gloom
> Our peace branch from above.
> "Then sorrow, touched by Thee,
> grows bright,
> With more than rapture's ray;

As darkness shows us worlds of
light
We never saw by day."

Of course it may be conceded that some troubles are really imaginary. They have no existence other than in the mind. Some are anticipated troubles, which never arrive at our door. Others are past troubles, and there is much folly in worrying over them. Present troubles are the ones requiring attention and demanding prayer. "Sufficient unto the day is the evil thereof." Some troubles are self-originated. We are their authors. Some of these originate involuntarily with us, some arise from our ignorance, some come from our carelessness. All this can be readily admitted without breaking the force of the statement that they are the subjects of prayer, and should drive us to prayer. What father casts off his child who cries to him when the little one from its own carelessness has stumbled and fallen and hurt itself? Does not the cry of the child attract the ears of the father even though the child be to blame for the accident? "Whatever things ye desire" takes in every event of life, even though some events we are responsible for.

Some troubles are human in their origin. They arise from second causes. They originate with others and we are the sufferers. This is a world where often the innocent suffer the consequences of the acts of others. This is a part of life's incidents. Who has not at some time suffered at the hands of others? But even these are allowed to come in the order of God's providence, are permitted to break into our lives for beneficent ends, and may be prayed over. Why should we not carry our hurts, our wrongs and our privations, caused by the acts of others, to God in prayer? Are such things outside of the realm of prayer? Are they exceptions to the rule of prayer? Not at all. And God can and will lay His hand upon all such events in answer to prayer, and cause them to work for us "a far more exceeding and eternal weight of glory."

Nearly all of Paul's troubles arose from wicked and unreasonable men. Read the story as he gives it in 2 Cor. 11:23-33.

So also some troubles are directly of Satanic origin. Quite all of Job's troubles were the offspring of the devil's scheme to break down Job's integrity, to make him charge God foolishly and to curse God. But are these not to be recognised in prayer? Are they to be excluded from God's disciplinary processes? Job did not do so. Hear him in those familiar words. "The Lord gave, and the Lord hath taken away. Blessed be the name of the Lord"

Owhat a comfort to see God in all of life's events! What a relief to a broken, sorrowing heart to see God's hand in sorrow! What a source of relief is prayer in unburdening the heart in grief!

"O Thou who driest the mourner's
    tear,
How dark this world would be,
If, when deceived and wounded
    here,
We could not fly to Thee?
"The friends who in our sunshine
    live,
When winter comes are flown,
And he who has but tears to give,
Must weep those tears alone.
"But Thou wilt heal the broken
    heart,
Which, like the plants that throw
Their fragrance from the wounded
    part,
Breathes sweetness out of woe."

But when we survey all the sources from which trouble comes, it all resolves itself into two invaluable truths: First, that our troubles at last are of the Lord. They come with His consent He is in all of them, and is interested in us when they press and bruise us. And secondly, that our troubles, no matter what the cause, whether of ourselves, or men or devils, or even God Himself, we are warranted in taking them to God in prayer, in praying over them, and in seeking to get the greatest spiritual benefits out of them.

Prayer in the time of trouble tends to bring the spirit into perfect subjection to the will of God, to cause the will to be conformed to God's will, and saves from all murmurings over our lot, and delivers from everything like a rebellious heart or a spirit critical of the Lord. Prayer sanctifies trouble to our highest good. Prayer so prepares the heart that it softens under the disciplining hand of God. Prayer places us where God can bring to us the greatest good, spiritual and eternal. Prayer allows God to freely work with us and in us in the day of trouble. Prayer removes everything in the way of trouble, bringing to us the sweetest, the highest and greatest good. Prayer permits God's servant, trouble, to accomplish its mission in us, with us and for us.

The end of trouble is always good in the mind of God. If trouble fails in its mission, it is either because of prayerlessness or unbelief, or both. Being in harmony with God in the dispensations of His providence, always makes trouble a blessing. The good or evil of trouble is always determined by the spirit in which it is received. Trouble proves a blessing or a curse, just according as it is received and treated by us. It either softens or hardens us. It either draws us to prayer and to God or it drives us from God and from the closet. Trouble hardened Pharaoh till finally it had no effect on him, only to make him more desperate and to drive him farther from God. The same sun softens the wax and hardens the clay. The same sun melts the ice and dries out the moisture from the earth.

As is the infinite variety of trouble, so also is there infinite variety in the relations of prayer to other things. How many are the things which are the subject of prayer! It has to do with everything which concerns us, with everybody with whom we have to do, and has to do with all times. But especially does prayer have to do with trouble. "This poor man cried and the Lord heard him, and saved him out of all his troubles." O the blessedness, the help, the comfort of prayer in the day of trouble! And how marvelous the promises of God to us in the time of trouble!

"Because he hath set his love upon me, therefore will I deliver him; I will set him on high because he hath known my name. He shall call upon me, and I will answer him; I will be with him in trouble; I will deliver him and honor him."

> "If pain afflict, or wrongs oppress,
> If cares distract, or fears dismay;
> If guilt deject, if sin distress,
> In every case, still watch and pray."

How rich in its sweetness, how far-reaching in the realm of trouble, and how cheering to faith, are the words of promise which God delivers to His believing, praying ones, by the mouth of Isaiah:

"*But now, thus saith the Lord that created thee, O Jacob, and he that formed thee, O Israel, Fear not: for I have redeemed thee, I have called thee by thy name; thou art mine. When thou passest through the waters, I will be with thee; and through the rivers, they shall not overflow thee: when thou walkest through the fire, thou shalt not be burned: neither shall the flame kindle upon thee . . . For I am the Lord thy God, the Holy One of Israel, thy Saviour.*"

Chapter 6

PRAYER AND TROUBLE
(Continued)

In the New Testament there are three words used which embrace trouble. These are tribulation, suffering and affliction, words differing somewhat, and yet each of them practically meaning trouble of some kind. Our Lord put His disciples on notice that they might expect tribulation in this life, teaching them that tribulation belonged to this world, and they could not hope to escape it; that they would not be carried through this life on flowery beds of ease. How hard to learn this plain and patent lesson! "In the world ye shall have tribulation; but be of good cheer; I have overcome the world." There is the encouragement. As He had overcome the world and its tribulations, so might they do the same.

Paul taught the same lesson throughout his ministry, when in confirming the souls of the brethren, and exhorting them to continue in the faith, he told them that "we must, through much tribulation, enter into the kingdom of God." He himself knew this by his own experience, for his pathway was anything but smooth and flowery.

He it is who uses the word "suffering" to describe the troubles of life, in that comforting passage in which he contrasts life's troubles with the final glory of heaven, which shall be the reward of all who patiently endure the ills of Divine Providence:

"For I reckon that the sufferings of this present time are not worthy to be compared with the glory which shall be revealed in us."

And he it is who speaks of the afflictions which come to the people of God in this world, and regards them as light as compared with the weight of glory awaiting all who are submissive, patient and faithful in all their troubles:

"For our light affliction, which is but for a moment, worketh for us a far more exceeding and eternal weight of glory."

But these present afflictions can work for us only as we cooperate with God in prayer. As God works through prayer, it is only through this means He can accomplish His highest ends for us. His Providence works with greatest effect with His praying ones. These know the uses of trouble and its gracious designs. The greatest value in trouble comes to those who bow lowest before the throne.

Paul, in urging patience in tribulation, connects it directly with prayer, as if prayer alone would place us where we could be patient when tribulation comes. "Rejoicing in hope, patient in tribulation, continuing instant in prayer." He here couples up tribulation and prayer, showing their close relationship and the worth of prayer in begetting and culturing patience in tribulation. In fact there can be no patience exemplified when trouble comes, only as it is secured through instant and continued prayer. In the school of prayer is where patience is learned and practiced.

Prayer brings us into that state of grace where tribulation is not only endured, but where there is under it a spirit of rejoicing. In showing the gracious benefits of justification, in Romans 5:3, Paul says:

"And not only so, but we glory in tribulation also: knowing that tribulation worketh patience; and patience, experience; and experience, hope; and hope maketh not ashamed; because the love of God is shed abroad in our hearts by the Holy Ghost which is given unto us."

What a chain of graces are here set forth as flowing from tribulation! What successive steps to a high state of religious experience! And what rich fruits result from even painful tribulation!

To the same effect are the words of Peter in his First Epistle, in his strong prayer for those Christians to whom he writes; thus showing that suffering and the highest state of grace are closely connected; and intimating that it is through suffering we are to be brought to those higher regions of Christian experience:

"But the God of all grace, who hath called us into his eternal glory, by Christ Jesus, after that ye have suffered awhile, make you perfect, stablish, strengthen and settle you."

It is in the fires of suffering that God purifies His saints and brings them to the highest things. It is in the furnace their faith is tested, their patience is tried, and they are developed in all those rich virtues which make up Christian character. It is while they are passing through deep waters that He shows how close He can come to His praying, believing saints.

It takes faith of a high order and a Christian experience far above the average religion of this day, to count it joy when we are called to pass through tribulation. God's highest aim in dealing with His people is in developing Christian character. He is after begetting in us those rich virtues which belong to our Lord Jesus Christ. He is seeking to make us like Himself. It is not so much work that He wants in us. It is not greatness. It is the presence in us of patience, meekness, submission to the Divine will, prayerfulness which brings everything to Him. He seeks to beget His own image in us. And trouble in some form tends to do this very thing, for this is the end and aim of trouble. This is its work. This is the task it is called to perform. It is not a chance incident in life, but has a design in view, just as it has an All-wise Designer back of it, who makes trouble His agent to bring forth the largest results.

The writer of the Epistle to the Hebrews gives us a perfect directory of trouble, comprehensive, clear and worth while to be studied. Here is "chastisement," another word for trouble, coming from a Father's hand, showing God is in all the sad and afflictive events of life. Here is its nature and its gracious design. It is not punishment in the accurate meaning of that word, but the means God employs to correct and discipline His children in dealing with them on earth. Then we have the fact of the evidence of being His people, namely, the presence of chastisement. The ultimate end is that we "may be partakers of his holiness," which is but another way of saying that all this disciplinary process is to the end that God may make us like Himself. What an encouragement, too, that, chastisement is no evidence of anger or displeasure on God's part, but is the strong proof of His love. Let us read the entire directory on this important subject:

"And ye have forgotten the exhortation which speaketh unto you as unto children, My son, despise

not thou the chastening of the Lord, nor faint when thou art rebuked of him: For whom the Lord loveth he chasteneth, and scourgeth every son whom he receiveth. If ye endure chastening, God dealeth with you as with sons; for what son is he whom the father chasteneth not? But if ye are without chastisement, whereof all are partakers, then are ye bastards and not sons.

"Furthermore, we have had fathers of our flesh which corrected us, and we gave them reverence: shall we not much rather be in subjection to the Father of spirits and live? For they verily for a few days chastened us after their own pleasure; but he for our profit, that we might be partakers of his holiness. Now no chastening for the present seemeth to be joyous, but grievous; nevertheless, afterward it yieldeth the peaceable fruit of righteousness to them which are exercised thereby."

Just as prayer is wide in its range, taking in everything, so trouble is infinitely varied in its uses and designs. It takes trouble sometimes to arrest attention, to stop men in the busy rush of life, and to awaken them to a sense of their helplessness and their need and sinfulness. Not till King Manasseh was bound with thorns and carried away into a foreign land and got into deep trouble, was he awakened and brought back to God. It was then he humbled himself and began to call upon God.

The Prodigal Son was independent and self-sufficient when in prosperity, but when money and friends departed, and he began to be in want, then it was he "came to himself," and decided to return to his father's house, with prayer and confession on his lips. Many a man who has forgotten God has been arrested, caused to consider his ways, and brought to remember God and pray by trouble. Blessed is trouble when it accomplishes this in men!

It is for this among other reasons that Job says:

"Behold, happy is the man whom God correcteth. Therefore, despise not thou the chastening of the Almighty. For he maketh sore, and bindeth up; he woundeth, and his hands maketh whole. He shall deliver thee in six troubles; yea, in seven there shall no evil touch thee."

One thing more might be named. Trouble makes earth undesirable and causes heaven to loom up large in the horizon of hope. There is a world where trouble never comes. But the path of tribulation leads to that world. Those who are there went there through tribulation. What a world set before our longing eyes which appeals to our hopes, as sorrows like a cyclone sweep over us! Hear John, as he talks about it and those who are there:

"What are these which are arrayed in white robes? and whence came they? . . . And he said to me, These are they which came out of great tribulation, and have washed their robes and made them white in

the blood of the Lamb . . . And God shall wipe away all tears from their eyes."

> "There I shall bathe my weary soul,
> In seas of heavenly rest,
> And not a wave of trouble roll,
> Across my peaceful breast."

Oh, children of God, ye who have suffered, who have been sorely tried, whose sad experiences have often brought broken spirits and bleeding hearts, cheer up! God is in all your troubles, and He will see that all shall "work together for good," if you will but be patient, submissive and prayerful.

Chapter 7

PRAYER AND GOD'S WORK

God has a great work on hand in this world. This work is involved in the plan of salvation. It embraces redemption and providence. God is governing this world, with its intelligent beings, for His own glory and for their good. What, then, is God's work in this world? Rather what is the end He seeks in His great work? It is nothing short of holiness of heart and life in the children of fallen Adam. Man is a fallen creature, born with an evil nature, with an evil bent, unholy propensities, sinful desires, wicked inclinations. Man is unholy by nature, born so. "They go astray as soon as they be born, speaking lies."

God's entire plan is to take hold of fallen man and to seek to change him and make him holy.

God's work is to make holy men out of unholy men. This is the very end of Christ coming into the world:

"For this purpose was the Son of God manifested that he might destroy the works of the devil."

God is holy in nature and in all His ways, and He wants to make man like Himself.

"As he who hath called you is holy, so be ye holy in all manner of conversation; because it is written, Be ye holy, for I am holy."

This is being Christlike. This is following Jesus Christ. This is the aim of all Christian effort. This is the earnest, heartfelt desire of every truly regenerated soul. This is what is to be constantly and earnestly prayed for. It is that we may be made holy. Not that we must make ourselves holy, but we must be cleansed from all sin by the precious atoning blood of Christ, and be made holy by the direct agency of the Holy Spirit. Not that we are to do holy, but rather to be holy. Being must precede doing. First be, then do. First, obtain a holy heart, then live a holy life. And for this high and gracious end God has made the most ample provisions in the atoning work of our Lord and through the agency of the Holy Spirit.

The work of God in the world is the implantation, the growth and the perfection of holiness in His people. Keep this ever in mind. But we might ask just now, Is this work advancing in the Church? Are men and women being made holy? Is the present-day Church engaged in the business of making holy men and women? This is not a vain and speculative question. It is practical, pertinent and all important.

The present-day Church has vast machinery. Her activities are great, and her material prosperity is unparalleled. The name of religion is widely-spread and well-known. Much money comes into the Lord's treasury and is paid out. But here is the question: Does the work of holiness keep pace with all this? Is the burden of the prayers of Church people to be made holy? Are our preachers really holy men? Or to go back a little further, are they hungering and thirsting after righteousness, desiring the sincere milk of the Word that they may grow thereby? Are they really seeking to be holy men? Of course men of intelligence are greatly needed in the pulpit, but prior to that, and primary to it, is the fact that we need holy men to stand before dying men and proclaim the salvation of God to them.

Ministers, like laymen, and no more so than laymen, must be holy men in life, in conversation and in temper. They must be examples to the flock of God in all things. By their lives they are to preach as well as to speak. Men in the pulpit are needed who are spotless in life, circumspect in behaviour, "without rebuke and blameless in the midst of a crooked and perverse nation, among whom they are to shine in the world." Are our preachers of this type of men? We are simply asking the question. Let the reader make up his own judgment. Is the work of holiness making progress among our preachers?

Again let us ask: Are our leading laymen examples of holiness? Are they seeking holiness of heart and life? Are they praying men, ever praying that God would fashion them according to His pattern of holiness? Are their business ways without stain of sin, and their gains free from the taint of wrong-doing? Have they the foundation of solid honesty, and does uprightness bring them into elevation and influence? Does business integrity and probity run parallel with religious activity, and with churchly observance?

Then, while we are pursuing our investigation, seeking light as to whether the work of God among His people is making progress, let us ask further as to our women. Are the leading women of our churches dead to the fashions of this world, separated from the world, not conformed to the world's maxims and customs? Are they in behaviour as becometh holiness, teaching the young women by word and life the lessons of soberness, obedience, and home-keeping? Are our women noted for their praying habits? Are they patterns of prayer?

How searching are all these questions? And

will any one dare say they are impertinent and out of place? If God's work be to make men and women holy, and He has made ample provisions in the law of prayer of doing this very thing, why should it be thought impertinent and useless to propound such personal and pointed questions as these? They have to do directly with the work and with its progress and its perfection. They go to the very seat of the disease. They hit the spot.

We might as well face the situation first as last. There is no use to shut our eyes to real facts. If the Church does not do this sort of work—if the Church does not advance its members in holiness of heart and life—then all our show of activities and all our display of Church work are a delusion and a snare.

But let us ask as to another large and important class of people in our churches. They are the hope of the future Church. To them all eyes are turned. Are our young men and women growing in sober-mindedness and reverence, and in all those graces which have their root in the renewed heart, which mark solid and permanent advance in the Divine life? If we are not growing in holiness, then we are doing nothing religious nor abiding.

Material prosperity is not the infallible sign of spiritual prosperity. The former may exist while the latter is significantly absent. Material prosperity may easily blind the eyes of Church leaders, so much so that they will make it a substitute for spiritual prosperity. How great the need to watch at that point! Prosperity in money matters does not signify growth in holiness. The seasons of material prosperity are rarely seasons of spiritual advance, either to the individual or to the Church. It is so easy to lose sight of God when goods increase. It is so easy to lean on human agencies and cease praying and relying upon God when material prosperity comes to the Church.

If it be contended that the work of God is progressing, and that we are growing in holiness, then some perplexing questions arise which will be hard to answer. If the Church is making advances on the lines of deep spirituality—if we are a praying people, noted for our prayer habits—if our people are hungering after holiness—then let us ask, why do we now have so few mighty outpourings of the Holy Spirit on our chief churches and our principal appointments? Why is it that so few of our revivals spring from the life of the pastor, who is noted for his deep spirituality, or the life of our church? Is the Lord's hand shortened that He cannot save? Is His ear heavy that He cannot hear? Why is it that in order to have so-called revivals, we must have outside pressure, by the reputation and sensation of some renowned evangelist? This is largely true in our larger charges and with our leading men. Why is it that the pastor is not sufficiently spiritual, holy and in communion with God, that he cannot hold his own revival services, and have large outpourings of the Holy Spirit on the Church, the community and upon himself? There can be but one solution for all this state of things. We have cultivated other things to the neglect of the work of holiness. We have permitted our minds to be preoccupied with material things in the Church. Unfortunately, whether designedly or not, we have substituted the external for the internal. We have put that which is seen to the front and shut out that which is unseen. It is all too true as to the Church, that we are much further advanced in material matters than in matters spiritual.

But the cause of this sad state of things may be traced further back. It is largely due to the decay of prayer. For with the decline of the work of holiness there has come the decline of the business of praying. As praying and holiness go together, so the decline of one, means the decay of the other. Excuse it if we may, justify the present state of things if we will, yet it is all too patent that the emphasis in the work of the present-day Church is not put on prayer. And just as this has occurred, the emphasis has been taken from the great work of God set on foot in the atonement, holiness of heart and life. The Church is not turning out praying men and women, because the Church is not intently engaged in the one great work of holiness.

At one time, John Wesley saw that there was a perceptible decline in the work of holiness, and he stopped short to inquire into the cause, and if we are as honest and spiritual as he was, we will now see the same causes operating to stay God's work among us. In a letter to his brother, Charles, at one time, he comes directly to the point, and makes short, incisive work of it. Here is how he begins his letter:

"What has hindered the work? I want to consider this. And must we not first say, we are the chief. If we were more holy in heart and life, thoroughly devoted to God, would not all the preachers catch fire, and carry it with them, throughout the land?

"Is not the next hindrance the littleness of grace (rather than of gifts) in a considerable part of our preachers? They have not the whole mind that was in Christ. They do not steadily walk as He walked. And, therefore, the hand of the Lord is stayed, though not altogether; though He does work still. But it is not in such a degree as He surely would, were they holy as He that hath sent them is holy.

"Is not the third hindrance the littleness of grace in the generality of our people? Therefore, they pray little, and with little fervency for a general blessing. And, therefore, their prayer has little power with God. It does not, as once, shut and open heaven.

"Add to this, that as there is much of the spirit of the world in their hearts, so there is much conformity to the world in their lives. They ought to be bright and shining lights, but they neither burn nor shine. They are not true to the rules they profess to observe. They are not holy in all manner of conversation. Nay, many of them are salt that has lost its savour, the little savour they once had. Wherewith then shall the rest of the land be seasoned? What wonder that their neighbours are as unholy as ever?"

He strikes the spot. He hits the centre. He grades the cause. He freely confesses that he and Charles are the first cause, in this decline of holiness. The chief ones occupy positions of responsibility. As they go, so goes the Church. They give colour to the Church. They largely determine its character and its work. What holiness should mark these chief men? What zeal should ever characterise them? What prayerfulness should be seen in them! How influential they ought to be with God! If the head be weak, then the whole body will feel the stroke.

The pastors come next in his catalogue. When the chief shepherds and those who are under them, the immediate pastors, stay their advance in holiness, the panic will reach to the end of the line. As are the pastors, so will the people be as a rule. If the pastors are prayerless, then will the people follow in their footsteps. If the preacher be silent upon the work of holiness, then will there be no hungering and thirsting after holiness in the laymen. If the preacher be careless about obtaining the highest and best God has for him in religious experience, then will the people take after him.

One statement of Wesley needs to be repeated with emphasis. The littleness of grace, rather than the smallness of gifts,—this is largely the case with the preachers. It may be stated as an axiom: That the work of God fails as a general rule, more for the lack of grace, than for the want of gifts. It is more than this. It is more than this, for a full supply of grace brings an increase of gifts. It may be repeated that small results, a low experience, a low religious life, and pointless, powerless preaching always flow from a lack of grace. And a lack of grace flows from a lack of praying. Great grace comes from great praying.

> "What is our calling's glorious hope
> But inward holiness?
> For this to Jesus I look up,
> I calmly wait for this.
> "I wait till He shall touch me clean,
> Shall life and power impart;
> Give me the faith that casts out sin,
> And purifies the heart."

In carrying on His great work in the world, God

works through human agents. He works through His Church collectively and through His people individually. In order that they may be effective agents, they must be "vessels unto honour, sanctified, and meet for the Master's use, and prepared unto every good work." God works most effectively through holy men. His work makes progress in the hands of praying men. Peter tells us that husbands who might not be reached by the Word of God, might be won by the conversation of their wives. It is those who are "blameless and harmless, the sons of God," who can hold forth the word of life "in the midst of a crooked and perverse nation."

The world judges religion not by what the Bible says, but by how Christians live. Christians are the Bible which sinners read. These are the epistles to be read of all men. "By their fruits ye shall know them." The emphasis, then, is to be placed upon holiness of life. But unfortunately in the present-day Church, emphasis has been placed elsewhere. In selecting Church workers and choosing ecclesiastical officers, the quality of holiness is not considered. The praying fitness seems not to be taken into account, when it was just otherwise in all of God's movements and in all of His plans. He looked for holy men, those noted for their praying habits. Prayer leaders are scarce. Prayer conduct is not counted as the highest qualification for offices in the Church.

We cannot wonder that so little is accomplished in the great work in the world which God has in hand. The fact is that it is surprising so much has been done with such feeble, defective agents. "Holiness to the Lord" needs again to be written on the banners of the Church. Once more it needs to be sounded out in the ears of modern Christians. "Follow peace with all men, and holiness, without which no man shall see the Lord."

Let it be iterated and reiterated that this is the Divine standard of religion. Nothing short of this will satisfy the Divine requirement. O the danger of deception at this point! How near one can come to being right and yet be wrong! Some men can come very near to pronouncing the test word, "Shibboleth," but they miss it "Many will say unto me, Lord, Lord, in that day," says Jesus Christ, but He further states that then will He say unto them, "I never knew you; depart from me, ye that work iniquity."

Men can do many good things and yet not be holy in heart and righteous in conduct. They can do many good things and lack that spiritual quality of heart called holiness. How great the need of hearing the words of Paul guarding us against self-deception in the great work of personal salvation:

"Be not deceived; God is not mocked: for whatsoever a man soweth, that shall he also reap."

"O may I still from sin depart;
A wise and understanding heart,
Jesus, to me to be given;
And let me through thy Spirit know
To glorify my God below,
And find my way to heaven."

Chapter 8

PRAYER AND CONSECRATION

When we study the many-sidedness of prayer, we are surprised at the number of things with which it is connected. There is no phase of human life which it does not affect, and it has to do with everything affecting human salvation. Prayer and consecration are closely related. Prayer leads up to, and governs consecration. Prayer is precedent to consecration, accompanies it, and is a direct result of it. Much goes under the name of consecration which has no consecration in it. Much consecration of the present day is defective, superficial and spurious, worth nothing so far as the office and ends of consecration are concerned. Popular consecration is sadly at fault because it has little or no prayer in it. No consecration is worth a thought which is not the direct fruit of much praying, and which fails to bring one into a life of prayer. Prayer is the one thing prominent in a consecrated life.

Consecration is much more than a life of so-called service. It is a life of personal holiness, first of all. It is that which brings spiritual power into the heart and enlivens the entire inner man. It is a life which ever recognises God, and a life given up to true prayer.

Full consecration is the highest type of a Christian life. It is the one Divine standard of experience, of living and of service. It is the one thing at which the believer should aim. Nothing short of entire consecration must satisfy him.

Never is he to be contented till he is fully, entirely the Lord's by his own consent. His praying naturally and involuntarily leads up to this one act of his.

Consecration is the voluntary set dedication of one's self to God, an offering definitely made, and made without any reservation whatever. It is the setting apart of all we are, all we have, and all we expect to have or be, to God first of all. It is not so much the giving of ourselves to the Church, or the mere engaging in some one line of Church work. Almighty God is in view and He is the end of all consecration. It is a separation of one's self to God, a devotement of all that he is and has to a sacred use. Some things may be devoted to a special purpose, but it is not consecration in the true sense. Consecration has a sacred nature. It is devoted to holy ends. It is the voluntary putting of one's self in God's hands to be used sacredly, holily, with sanctifying ends in view.

Consecration is not so much the setting one's self apart from sinful things and wicked ends, but rather it is the separation from worldly, secular and even legitimate things, if they come in conflict with God's plans, to holy uses. It is the devoting of all we have to God for His own specific use. It is a separation from things questionable, or even legitimate, when the choice is to be made between the things of this life and the claims of God.

The consecration which meets God's demands and which He accepts is to be full, complete, with no mental reservation, with nothing withheld. It cannot be partial, any more than a whole burnt offering in Old Testament times could have been partial. The whole animal had to be offered in sacrifice. To reserve any part of the animal would have seriously vitiated the offering. So to make a half-hearted, partial consecration is to make no consecration at all, and is to fail utterly in securing the Divine acceptance. It involves our whole being, all we have and all that we are. Everything is definitely and voluntarily placed in God's hands for His supreme use.

Consecration is not all there is in holiness.

Many make serious mistakes at this point. Consecration makes us relatively holy. We are holy only in the sense that we are now closely related to God, in which we were not related heretofore Consecration is the human side of holiness. In this sense, it is self-sanctification, and only in this sense. Sanctification or holiness in its truest and highest sense is Divine, the act of the Holy Spirit working in the heart, making it clean and putting therein in a higher degree the fruits of the Spirit.

This distinction is clearly set forth and kept in view by Moses in "Leviticus," wherein he shows the human and the Divine side of sanctification or holiness:

"Sanctify yourselves, therefore, and be ye holy, for I am the Lord your God. And ye shall keep my statutes and do them; I am the Lord which sanctify you."

Here we are to sanctify ourselves, and then in the next word we are taught that it is the Lord which sanctifies us. God does not consecrate us to His service. We do not sanctify ourselves in this highest sense. Here is the two-fold meaning of sanctification, and a distinction which needs to be always kept in mind.

Consecration being the intelligent, voluntary act of the believer, this act is the direct result of praying. No prayerless man ever conceives the idea of a full consecration. Prayerlessness and consecration have nothing whatever in common. A life of prayer naturally leads up to full consecration. It leads nowhere else. In fact, a life of prayer is satisfied with nothing else but an entire dedication of one's self to God. Consecration recognises fully God's ownership to us. It cheerfully assents to the truth set forth by Paul:

"Ye are not your own. For ye are bought with a price. Therefore, glorify God in your body and spirit, which are God's."

And true praying leads that way. It cannot reach any other destination. It is bound to run into this depot. This is its natural result This is the sort of work which praying turns out. Praying makes consecrated people. It cannot make any other sort. It drives to this end. It aims at this very purpose.

As prayer leads up to and brings forth full consecration, so prayer entirely impregnates a consecrated life. The prayer life and the consecrated life are intimate companions. They are Siamese twins, inseparable. Prayer enters into every phase of a consecrated life. A prayerless life which claims consecration is a misnomer, false, counterfeit.

Consecration is really the setting apart of one's self to a life of prayer. It means not only to pray, but to pray habitually, and to pray more effectually. It is the consecrated man who accomplishes most by His praying. God must hear the man wholly given up to God. God cannot deny the requests of him who has renounced all claims to himself, and who has wholly dedicated himself to God and His service. This act of the consecrated man puts him "on praying ground and pleading terms" with God. It puts Him in reach of God in prayer. It places him where he can get hold of God, and where he can influence God to do things which He would not otherwise do. Consecration brings answers to prayer. God can depend upon consecrated men. God can afford to commit Himself in prayer to those who have fully committed themselves to God. He who gives all to God will get all from God. Having given all to God, he can claim all that God has for him.

As prayer is the condition of full consecration, so prayer is the habit, the rule, of him who has dedicated himself wholly to God. Prayer is becoming in the consecrated life. Prayer is no strange thing in such a life. There is a peculiar affinity between prayer and consecration, for both recognise God, both submit to God, and both have their aim and end in God. Prayer is part and parcel of the consecrated life. Prayer is the constant, the inseparable, the intimate companion of consecration. They walk and talk together.

There is much talk today of consecration, and many are termed consecrated people who know not the alphabet of it. Much modern consecration falls far below the Scripture standard. There is really no real consecration in it. Just as there is much praying without any real prayer in it, so there is much so-called consecration current, today, in the Church which has no real consecration in it. Much for consecration in the Church which receives the praise and plaudits of superficial, formal professors, but which is wide of the mark. There is much hurrying to and fro, here and there, much fuss and feathers, much going about and doing many things, and those who busy themselves after this fashion are called consecrated men and women. The central trouble with all this false consecration is that there is no prayer in it, nor is it in any sense the direct result of praying. People can do many excellent and commendable things in the Church and be utter strangers to a life of consecration, just as they can do many things and be prayerless.

Here is the true test of consecration. It is a life of prayer. Unless prayer be pre-eminent, unless prayer is to the front, the consecration is faulty, deceptive, falsely named. Does he pray? That is the test-question of every so-called consecrated man. Is he a man of prayer? No consecration is worth a thought if it be devoid of prayer. Yea, more—if it be not pre-eminently and primarily a life of prayer.

God wants consecrated men because they can pray and will pray. He can use consecrated men because He can use praying men. As prayerless men are in His way, hinder Him, and prevent the success of His cause, so likewise unconsecrated men are useless to Him, and hinder Him in carrying out His gracious plans, and in executing His noble purposes in redemption. God wants consecrated men because He wants praying men. Consecration and prayer meet in the same man. Prayer is the tool with which the consecrated man works. Consecrated men are the agents through whom prayer works. Prayer helps the consecrated man in maintaining his attitude of consecration, keeps him alive to God, and aids him in doing the work to which he is called and to which he has given himself. Consecration helps to effectual praying. Consecration enables one to get the most out of his praying.

> "Let Him to whom we now belong
> His sovereign right assert;
> And take up every thankful song,
> And every loving heart.
> "He justly claims us for His own,
> Who bought us with a price;
> The Christian lives to Christ alone,
> To Christ alone he dies."

We must insist upon it that the prime purpose of consecration is not service in the ordinary sense of that word. Service in the minds of not a few means nothing more than engaging in some of the many forms of modern Church activities. There are a multitude of such activities, enough to engage the time and mind of anyone, yea, even more than enough. Some of these may be good, others not so good. The present-day Church is filled with machinery, organisations, committees and societies, so much so that the power it has is altogether insufficient to run the machinery, or to furnish life sufficient to do all this external work. Consecration has a much higher and nobler end than merely to expend itself in these external things.

Consecration aims at the right sort of service—the Scriptural kind. It seeks to serve God, but in entirely a different sphere than that which is in the minds of present-day Church leaders and workers. The very first sort of service mentioned by Zachariah, father of John the Baptist, in his wonderful prophecy and statement in Luke 1:74, was thus:

"That he would grant unto us, that we, being delivered out of the hand of our enemies, might serve him without fear, in holiness and righteousness, all the days of our life."

Here we have the idea of "serving God in holiness and righteousness all the days of our life."

And the same kind of service is mentioned in Luke's strong tribute to the father and mother of John the Baptist before the latter's birth:

"And they were both righteous before God,

walking in all the commandments and ordinances of the Lord blameless."

And Paul, in writing to the Philippians, strikes the same keynote in putting the emphasis on blamelessness of life:

"Do all things without murmurings and disputings, that ye may be blameless and harmless, the sons of God without rebuke, in the midst of a crooked and perverse nation, among whom ye shine as lights in the world; holding forth the word of life."

We must mention a truth which is strangely overlooked in these days by what are called personal workers, that in the Epistles of Paul and others, it is not what are called Church activities which are brought to the front, but rather the personal life. It is good behaviour, righteous conduct, holy living, godly conversation, right tempers—things which belong primarily to the personal life in religion. Everywhere this is emphasised, put in the forefront, made much of and insisted on. Religion first of all puts one to living right. Religion shows itself in the life. Thus is religion to prove its reality, its sincerity and its Divinity.

> "So let our lips and lives express
> The holy Gospel we profess;
> So let our works and virtues shine
> To prove the doctrine all Divine.

"Thus shall we best proclaim
abroad
The honors of our Saviour God;
When the salvation reigns within
And grace subdues the power of
sin."

The first great end of consecration is holiness of heart and of life. It is to glorify God, and this can be done in no more effectual way than by a holy life flowing from a heart cleansed from all sin. The great burden of heart pressed on every one who becomes a Christian lies right here. This he is to ever keep in mind, and to further this kind of life and this kind of heart, he is to watch, to pray, and to bend all his diligence in using all the means of grace. He who is truly and fully consecrated, lives a holy life. He seeks after holiness of heart. Is not satisfied without it. For this very purpose he consecrates himself to God. He gives himself entirely over to God in order to be holy in heart and in life.

As holiness of heart and of life is thoroughly impregnated with prayer, so consecration and prayer are closely allied in personal religion. It takes prayer to bring one into such a consecrated life of holiness to the Lord, and it takes prayer to maintain such a life. Without much prayer, such a life of holiness will break down. Holy people are praying people.

Holiness of heart and life puts people to praying. Consecration puts people to praying in earnest.

Prayerless people are strangers to anything like holiness of heart and cleanness of heart. Those who are unfamiliar with the closet are not at all interested in consecration and holiness. Holiness thrives in the place of secret prayer. The environments of the closet of prayer are favourable to its being and its culture. In the closet holiness is found. Consecration brings one into holiness of heart, and prayer stands hard by when it is done.

The spirit of consecration is the spirit of prayer. The law of consecration is the law of prayer. Both laws work in perfect harmony without the slightest jar or discord. Consecration is the practical expression of true prayer. People who are consecrated are known by their praying habits. Consecration thus expresses itself in prayer. He who is not interested in prayer has no interest in consecration. Prayer creates an interest in consecration, then prayer brings one into a state of heart where consecration is a subject of delight, bringing joy of heart, satisfaction of soul, contentment of spirit. The consecrated soul is the happiest soul. There is no friction whatever between him who is fully given over to God and God's will. There is perfect harmony between the will of such a man and God, and His will. And the two wills being in perfect accord, this brings rest of soul, absence of friction, and the presence of perfect peace.

> "Lord, in the strength of grace,
> With a glad heart and free,
> Myself, my residue of days,
> I consecrate to Thee.
> "Thy ransomed servant, I
> Restore to Thee Thy own;
> And from this moment, live or die,
> To serve my God alone."

Chapter 9

PRAYER AND A DEFINITE RELIGIOUS STANDARD

Much of the feebleness, barrenness and paucity of religion results from the failure to have a Scriptural and reasonable standard in religion, by which to shape character and measure results; and this largely results from the omission of prayer or the failure to put prayer in the standard. We cannot possibly mark our advances in religion if there is no point to which we are definitely advancing. Always there must be something definite before the mind's eye at which we are aiming and to which we are driving. We cannot contrast shapeliness with unshapeliness if there be no pattern after which to model. Neither can there be inspiration if there be no high end to stimulate us.

Many Christians are disjointed and aimless because they have no pattern before them after which conduct and character are to be shaped. They just move on aimlessly, their minds in a cloudy state, no pattern in view, no point in sight, no standard after which they are striving. There is no standard by which to value and gauge their efforts. No magnet is there to fill their eyes, quicken their steps, and to draw them and keep them steady.

All this vague idea of religion grows out of loose notions about prayer. That which helps to make the standard of religion clear and definite is prayer. That which aids in placing that standard high is prayer. The praying ones are those who have something definite in view. In fact prayer itself is a very definite thing, aims at something specific, and has a mark at which it aims. Prayer aims at the most definite, the highest and the sweetest religious experience. The praying ones want all that God has in store for them. They are not satisfied with anything like a low religious life, superficial, vague and indefinite. The praying ones are not only after a "deeper work of grace," but want the very deepest work of grace possible and promised. They are not after being saved from some sin, but saved from all sin, both inward and outward. They are after not only deliverance from sinning, but from sin itself, from its being, its power and its pollution. They are after holiness of heart and life.

Prayer believes in, and seeks for the very highest

religious life set before us in the Word of God. Prayer is the condition of that life. Prayer points out the only pathway to such a life. The standard of a religious life is the standard of prayer. Prayer is so vital, so essential, so far-reaching, that it enters into all religion, and sets the standard clear and definite before the eye. The degree of our estimate of prayer fixes our ideas of the standard of a religious life. The standard of Bible religion is the standard of prayer. The more there is of prayer in the life, the more definite and the higher our notions of religion.

The Scriptures alone make the standard of life and experience. When we make our own standard, there is delusion and falsity for our desires, convenience and pleasure form the rule, and that is always a fleshly and a low rule. From it, all the fundamental principles of a Christly religion are left out. Whatever standard of religion which makes in it provision for the flesh, is unscriptural and hurtful.

Nor will it do to leave it to others to fix the standard of religion for us. When we allow others to make our standard of religion, it is generally deficient because in imitation, defects are transferred to the imitator more readily than virtues, and a second edition of a man is marred by its defects.

The most serious damage in thus determining what religion is by what others say, is in allowing current opinion, the contagion of example, the grade of religion current among us, to shape our religious opinions and characters. Adoniram Judson once wrote to a friend, "Let me beg you, not to rest contented with the commonplace religion that is now so prevalent."

Commonplace religion is pleasing to flesh and blood. There is no self-denial in it, no cross bearing, no self-crucifixion. It is good enough for our neighbours. Why should we be singular and straight-laced? Others are living on a low plane, on a compromising level, living as the world lives. Why should we be peculiar, zealous of good works? Why should we fight to win heaven while so many are sailing there on "flowery beds of ease"? Are the easy-going, careless, sauntering crowd, living prayerless lives, going to heaven? Is heaven a fit place for non-praying, loose living, ease loving people? That is the supreme question.

Paul gives the following caution about making for ourselves the jolly, pleasure-seeking religious company all about us the standard of our measurement:

"For we dare not make ourselves of the number, or compare ourselves with some that commend themselves; but they, measuring themselves by themselves, and comparing themselves among themselves, are not wise. But we will not boast of things without our measure, but according to the measure of the rule

which God hath distributed to us, a measure to reach even unto you."

No standard of religion is worth a moment's consideration which leaves prayer out of the account. No standard is worth any thought which does not make prayer the main thing in religion. So necessary is prayer, so fundamental in God's plan, so all important to everything like a religious life, that it enters into all Bible religion. Prayer itself is a standard, definite, emphatic, Scriptural. A life of prayer is the Divine rule. This is the pattern, just as our Lord, being a man of prayer, is the one pattern for us after whom to copy. Prayer fashions the pattern of a religious life. Prayer is the measure. Prayer molds the life.

The vague, indefinite, popular view of religion has no prayer in it. In its programme, prayer is entirely left out or put so low down and made so insignificant, that it hardly is worth mentioning. Man's standard of religion has no prayer about it.

It is God's standard at which we are to aim, not man's. It is not the opinions of men, not what they say, but what the Scriptures say. Loose notions of religion grow out of low notions of prayer. Prayerlessness begets loose, cloudy and indefinite views of what religion is. Aimless living and prayerlessness go hand in hand. Prayer sets something definite in the mind. Prayer seeks after something specific. The more definite our views as to the nature and need of prayer, the more definite will be our views of Christian experience and right living, and the less vague our views of religion. A low standard of religion lives hard by a low standard of praying.

Everything in a religious life depends upon being definite. The definiteness of our religious experiences and of our living will depend upon the definiteness of our views of what religion is and of the things of which it consists.

The Scriptures ever set before us the one standard of full consecration to God. This is the Divine rule. This is the human side of this standard. The sacrifice acceptable to God must be a complete one, entire, a whole burnt offering. This is the measure laid down in God's Word. Nothing less than this can be pleasing to God. Nothing half-hearted can please Him. "A living sacrifice," holy, and perfect in all its parts, is the measurement of our service to God. A full renunciation of self, a free recognition of God's right to us, and a sincere offering of all to Him—this is the Divine requirement. Nothing indefinite in that. Nothing is in that which is governed by the opinions of others or affected by how men live about us.

And while a life of prayer is embraced in such a full consecration, at the same time prayer leads up to the point where a complete consecration is made to God. Consecration is but the silent expression of prayer. And the highest religious standard is the measure of prayer and self-dedication to God. The prayer-life and the consecrated life are partners in religion. They are so closely allied they are never separated. The prayer life is the direct fruit of entire consecration to God, Prayer is the natural outflow of a really consecrated life. The measure of consecration is the measure of real prayer. No consecration is pleasing to God which is not perfect in all its parts, just as no burnt offering of a Jew was ever acceptable to God unless it was a "whole burnt offering." And a consecration of this sort, after this Divine measurement, has in it as a basic principle, the business of praying. Consecration is made to God. Prayer has to do with God. Consecration is putting one's self entirely at the disposal of God. And God wants and commands all His consecrated ones to be praying ones. This is the one definite standard at which we must aim. Lower than this we cannot afford to seek.

A Scriptural standard of religion includes a clear religious experience. Religion is nothing if not experimental. Religion appeals to the inner consciousness. It is an experience if anything at all, and an experience in addition to a religious life. There is the internal part of religion as well as the external. Not only are we to "work out our salvation with fear and trembling," but "it is God that worketh in us to will and do of His good pleasure." There is a "good work in you," as well as a life outside to be lived. The new birth is a definite Christian experience, proved by infallible marks, appealing to the inner consciousness. The witness of the Spirit is not an indefinite, vague something, but is a definite, clear inward assurance given by the Holy Spirit that we are the children of God. In fact everything belonging to religious experience is clear and definite, bringing conscious joy, peace and love. And this is the Divine standard of religion, a standard attained by earnest, constant prayer, and a religious experience kept alive and enlarged by the same means of prayer.

An end to be gained, to which effort is to be directed, is important in every pursuit in order to give unity, energy and steadiness to it. In the Christian life, such an end is all important. Without a high standard before us to be gained, for which we are earnestly seeking, lassitude will unnerve effort, and past experience will taint or exhale into mere sentiment, or be hardened into cold, loveless principle.

We must go on. "Therefore, leaving the principles of the doctrine of Christ, let us go on unto perfection." The present ground we occupy must be held by making advances, and all the future must be covered and brightened by it. In religion, we must not only go on. We must know where we are going to. This is all important. It is essential that in going on in religious experience, we have something definite in view, and strike out for that one point. To ever go on and not to know to which place we are going, is altogether too vague and indefinite, and is like a man who starts out on a journey and does not have any destination in view. It is important that we lose not sight of the starting point in a religious life, and that we measure the steps already trod. But it is likewise necessary that the end be kept in view and that the steps necessary to reach the standard be always in the eye.

Chapter 10

PRAYER BORN OF COMPASSION

We speak here more particularly of spiritual compassion, that which is born in a renewed heart, and which finds hospitality there. This compassion has in it the quality of mercy, is of the nature of pity, and moves the soul with tenderness of feeling for others. Compassion is moved at the sight of sin, sorrow and suffering. It stands at the other extreme to indifference of spirit to the wants and woes of others, and is far removed from insensibility and hardness of heart, in the midst of want and trouble and wretchedness. Compassion stands besides sympathy for others, is interested in them, and is concerned about them.

That which excites and develops compassion and puts it to work, is the sight of multitudes in want and distress, and helpless to relieve themselves. Helplessness especially appeals to compassion. Compassion is silent but does not remain secluded. It goes out at the sight of trouble, sin and need. Compassion runs out in earnest prayer, first of all, for those for whom it feels, and has a sympathy for them. Prayer for others is born of a sympathetic heart. Prayer is natural and almost spontaneous when compassion is begotten in the heart. Prayer belongs to the compassionate man.

There is a certain compassion which belongs to the natural man, which expends its force in simple gifts to those in need, not to be despised. But spiritual compassion, the kind born in a renewed heart, which is Christly in its nature, is deeper, broader and more prayerlike. Christly compassion always moves to prayer. This sort of compassion goes beyond the relief of mere bodily wants, and saying, "Be ye warmed—be ye clothed." It reaches deeper down and goes much farther.

Compassion is not blind. Rather we should say, that compassion is not born of blindness. He who has compassion of soul has eyes, first of all, to see the things which excite compassion. He who has no eyes to see the exceeding sinfulness of sin, the wants and woes of humanity, will never have compassion for humanity. It is written of our Lord that "when he saw the multitudes, he was moved with compassion on them." First, seeing the multitudes, with their hunger, their woes and their helpless condition, then compassion. Then prayer for the multitudes. Hard is he, and far from being Christlike, who sees the multitudes, and is unmoved at the sight of their sad state, their unhappiness and their peril. He has no heart of prayer for men.

Compassion may not always move men, but is always moved toward men. Compassion may not always turn men to God, but it will, and does, turn God to man. And where it is most helpless to relieve the needs of others, it can at least break out into prayer to God for others. Compassion is never indifferent, selfish, and forgetful of others. Compassion has alone to do with others. The fact that the multitudes were as sheep having no shepherd, was the one thing which appealed to our Lord's compassionate nature. Then their hunger moved Him, and the sight of the sufferings and diseases of these multitudes stirred the pity of His heart.

> "Father of mercies, send Thy grace
> All powerful from above,
> To form in our obedient souls
> The image of Thy love.
> "O may our sympathising breasts
> That generous pleasure know;
> Kindly to share in others' joy,
> And weep for others' woe."

But compassion has not alone to do with the

body and its disabilities and needs. The soul's distressing state, its needs and danger all appeal to compassion. The highest state of grace is known by the infallible mark of compassion for poor sinners. This sort of compassion belongs to grace, and sees not alone the bodies of men, but their immortal spirits, soiled by sin, unhappy in their condition without God, and in imminent peril of being forever lost. When compassion beholds this sight of dying men hurrying to the bar of God, then it is that it breaks out into intercessions for sinful men. Then it is that compassion speaks out after this fashion:

> "But feeble my compassion proves,
> And can but weep where most it
> loves;
> Thy own all saving arm employ,
> And turn these drops of grief to
> joy."

The Prophet Jeremiah declares this about God, giving the reason why sinners are not consumed by His wrath:

"It is of the Lord's mercies we are not consumed, because his compassion fail not."

And it is this Divine quality in us which makes us so much like God. So we find the Psalmist describing the righteous man who is pronounced blessed by God: "He is gracious and full of compassion, and righteous."

And as giving great encouragement to penitent praying sinners, the Psalmist thus records some of the striking attributes of the Divine character: "The Lord is gracious and full of compassion, slow to anger, and of great mercy."

It is no wonder, then, that we find it recorded several times of our Lord while on earth that "he was moved with compassion." Can any one doubt that His compassion moved Him to pray for those suffering, sorrowing ones who came across His pathway?

Paul was wonderfully interested in the religious welfare of his Jewish brethren, was concerned over them, and his heart was strangely warmed with tender compassion for their salvation, even though mistreated and sorely persecuted by them. In writing to the Romans, we hear him thus express himself:

"I say the truth in Christ, I lie not, my conscience also bearing me witness in the Holy Ghost, that I have great heaviness and continual sorrow in my heart; for I could wish that myself were accursed for my brethren, my kinsmen according to the flesh."

What marvellous compassion is here described for Paul's own nation! What wonder that a little later on he records his desire and prayer:

"Brethren, my heart's desire and prayer to God for Israel is that they might be saved."

We have an interesting case in Matthew which gives us an account of what excited so largely the compassion of our Lord at one time:

"But when he saw the multitudes, he was moved with compassion on them, because they fainted, and were scattered abroad, as sheep having no shepherd. Then saith he unto his disciples, The harvest truly is plenteous, but the labourers are few. Pray ye therefore the Lord of the harvest, that he will send forth labourers into his harvest."

It seems from parallel statements that our Lord had called His disciples aside to rest awhile, exhausted as He and they were by the excessive drafts on them, by the ceaseless contact with the persons who were ever coming and going, and by their exhaustive toil in ministering to the immense multitudes. But the multitudes precede Him, and instead of finding wilderness-solitude, quiet and repose, He finds great multitudes eager to see and hear, and to be healed. His compassions are moved. The ripened harvests need labourers. He did not call these labourers at once, by sovereign authority, but charges the disciples to betake themselves to God in prayer, asking Him to send forth labourers into His harvest.

Here is the urgency of prayer enforced by the compassions of our Lord. It is prayer born of compassion for perishing humanity. Prayer is pressed on the Church for labourers to be sent into the harvest of the Lord. The harvest will go to waste and perish without the labourers, while the labourers must be God-chosen, God-sent, and God commissioned. But God does not send these labourers into His harvest without prayer. The failure of the labourers is owing to the failure of prayer. The scarcity of labourers in the harvest is due to the fact that the Church fails to pray for labourers according to His command.

The ingathering of the harvests of earth for the granaries of heaven is dependent on the prayers of God's people. Prayer secures the labourers sufficient in quantity and in quality for all the needs of the harvest. God's chosen labourers, God's endowed labourers, and God's thrust-forth labourers, are the only ones who will truly go, filled with Christly compassion and endued with Christly power, whose going will avail, and these are secured by prayer. Christ's people on their knees with Christ's compassion in their hearts for dying men and for needy souls, exposed to eternal peril, is the pledge of labourers in numbers and character to meet the wants of earth and the purposes of heaven.

God is sovereign of the earth and of heaven, and the choice of labourers in His harvest He delegates to no one else. Prayer honours Him as sovereign and moves Him to His wise and holy selection. We will have to put prayer to the front ere the fields of paganism will be successfully tilled for Christ. God knows His men, and He likewise knows full well His work. Prayer gets God to send forth the best men and the most fit men and the men best qualified to work in the harvest. Moving the missionary cause by forces this side of God has been its bane, its weakness and its failure. Compassion for the world of sinners, fallen in Adam, but redeemed in Christ will move the Church to pray for them and stir the Church to pray the Lord of the harvest to send forth labourers into the harvest.

> "Lord of the harvest hear
> Thy needy servants' cry;
> Answer our faith's effectual prayer,
> And all our wants supply.
> "Convert and send forth more
> Into Thy Church abroad;
> And let them speak Thy word of
> power,
> As workers with their God."

What a comfort and what hope there is to fill our breasts when we think of one in Heaven who ever liveth to intercede for us, because "His compassion fails not!" Above everything else, we have a compassionate Saviour, one "who can have compassion on the ignorant, and on them who are out of the way, for that he himself is compassed about with infirmity." The compassion of our Lord well fits Him for being the Great High Priest of Adam's fallen, lost and helpless race.

And if He is filled with such compassion that it moves Him at the Father's right hand to intercede for us, then by every token we should have the same compassion on the ignorant and those out of the way, exposed to Divine wrath, as would move us to pray for them. Just in so far as we are compassionate will we be prayerful for others. Compassion does not expend its force in simply saying, "Be ye warmed; be ye clothed," but drives us to our knees in prayer for those who need Christ and His grace.

> "The Son of God in tears
> The wondering angels see;
> Be thou astonished, O my soul!
> He shed those tears for thee.
> "He wept that we might weep;
> Each sin demands a tear;
> In heaven alone no sin is found,
> And there's no weeping there."

Jesus Christ was altogether man. While He was the Divine Son of God yet at the same time, He was the human Son of God. Christ had a pre-eminently human side, and, here, compassion reigned. He was tempted in all points as we are, yet without sin. At one time how the flesh seems to have weakened under the fearful strain upon Him, and how He must have inwardly shrunk under the pain and pull! Looking up to heaven, He prays, "Father, save me from this hour." How the spirit nerves and holds —"but for this cause came I to this hour." Only he can solve this mystery who has followed His Lord in straits and gloom and pain, and realised that the "spirit is willing but the flesh is weak."

All this but fitted our Lord to be a compassionate Saviour. It is no sin to feel the pain and realise the darkness on the path into which God leads. It is only human to cry out against the pain, the terror, and desolation of that hour. It is Divine to cry out to God in that hour, even while shrinking and sinking down, "For this cause came I unto this hour." Shall I fail through the weakness of the flesh? No. "Father, glorify thy name." How strong it makes us, and how true, to have one pole star to guide us to the glory of God!

Chapter 11

CONCERTED PRAYER

The pious Quesnel says that "God is found in union and agreement. Nothing is more efficacious than this in prayer."

Intercessions combine with prayers and supplications. The word does not mean necessarily prayer in relation to others. It means a coming together, a falling in with a most intimate friend for free, unrestrained communion. It implies prayer, free, familiar and bold.

Our Lord deals with this question of the concert of prayer in the eighteenth chapter of Matthew. He deals with the benefit and energy resulting from the aggregation of prayer forces. The prayer principle and the prayer promise will be best understood in the connection in which it was made by our Lord:

"Moreover, if thy brother shall trespass against thee, go and tell him his fault between thee and him alone: if he shall hear thee, thou hast gained thy brother. But if he will not hear thee, then take with thee one or two more, that in the mouth of two or three witnesses, every word may be established.

"And if he shall neglect to hear them, tell it unto the church; but if he neglect to hear the church, let him be unto thee as an heathen and a publican.

"Verily I say unto you, whatsoever ye shall bind on earth, shall be bound in heaven; and whatsoever ye shall loose on earth, shall be loosed in heaven. Again I say unto you, That if two of you shall agree on earth as touching any thing that they shall ask, it shall be done for them of my Father which is in heaven. For where two or three are gathered together in my name, there am I in the midst of them."

This represents the Church in prayer to enforce discipline in order that its members who have been overtaken by faults, may yield readily to the disciplinary process. In addition, it is the Church called together in a concert of prayer in order to repair the waste and friction ensuing upon the cutting off of a Church offender. This last direction as to a concert of prayer is that the whole matter may be referred to Almighty God for His approval and ratification.

All this means that the main, the concluding and the all powerful agency in the Church is prayer, whether it be, as we have seen in Matthew 9, to thrust out labourers into God's earthly harvest fields, or to exclude from the Church a violator of unity, law and order, who will neither listen to his brethren nor repent and confess his fault.

It means that Church discipline, now a lost art in the modern Church, must go hand in hand with prayer, and that the Church which has no disposition to separate wrong doers from the Church, and which has no excommunication spirit for incorrigible offenders against law and order, will have no communication with God. Church purity must precede the Church's prayers. The unity of discipline in the Church precedes the unity of prayers by the Church.

Let it be noted with emphasis that a Church which is careless of discipline will be careless in praying. A Church which tolerates evil doers in its communion, will cease to pray, will cease to pray with agreement, and will cease to be a Church gathered together in prayer in Christ's name.

This matter of Church discipline is an important one in the Scriptures. The need of watchfulness over the lives of its members belongs to the Church of God. The Church is an organization for mutual help, and it is charged with the watch care of all of its members. Disorderly conduct cannot be passed by unnoticed. The course of procedure in such cases is clearly given in the eighteenth chapter of Matthew, which has been heretofore referred to. Furthermore, Paul, in Galatians 6:1, gives explicit directions as to those who fall into sin in the Church:

"Brethren, if a man be overtaken in a fault, ye which are spiritual restore such a one in the spirit of meekness, considering thyself lest thou also be tempted."

The work of the Church is not alone to seek members but it is to watch over and guard them after they have entered the Church. And if any are overtaken by sin; they must be sought out, and if they cannot be cured of their faults, then excision must take place. This is the doctrine our Lord lays down.

It is somewhat striking that the Church at Ephesus, (Rev. 2) though it had left its first love, and had sadly declined in vital godliness and in those things which make up spiritual life, yet it receives credit for this good quality: "Thou canst not bear them that are evil."

While the Church at Pergamos was admonished because it had there among its membership those who taught such hurtful doctrines that were a stumbling-block to others. And not so much that such characters were in the Church, but that they were tolerated. The impression is that the Church leaders were blind to the presence of such hurtful characters, and hence were indisposed to administer discipline. This indisposition was an unfailing sign of prayerlessness in the membership. There was no union of prayer effort looking to cleansing the Church and keeping it clean.

This disciplinary idea stands out prominently in the Apostle Paul's writings to the Churches. The Church at Corinth had a notorious case of fornication where a man had married his step-mother, and this Church had been careless about this iniquity. Paul rather sharply reproved this Church and gave explicit command to this effect: "Therefore put away from among yourselves that wicked person" Here was concert of action on the part of praying people demanded by Paul.

As good a Church as that at Thessalonica needed instruction and caution on this matter of looking after disorderly persons. So we hear Paul saying unto them:

"Now we command you, brethren, in the name of our Lord Jesus Christ, that ye withdraw yourselves from every brother that walketh disorderly."

Mark you. It is not the mere presence of disorderly persons in a Church which merits the displeasure of God. It is when they are tolerated under the mistaken plea of "bearing with them," and no steps are taken either to cure them of their evil practices or exclude them from the fellowship of the Church. And this glaring neglect on the part of the Church of its wayward members, is but a sad sign of a lack of praying, for a praying Church, given to mutual praying, agreement praying, is keen to discern when a brother is overtaken in a fault, and seeks either to restore him, or to cut him off if he be incorrigible.

Much of this dates back to the lack of spiritual vision on the part of Church leaders. The Lord by the mouth of the Prophet Isaiah once asked the very pertinent, suggestive question, "And who is blind but my servant?" This blindness in leadership in the Church is no more patent than in this question of seeing evil doers in the Church, in caring for them, and when the effort to restore them fails, to withdraw fellowship from them and let them be "as a heathen man and a publican." The truth is there is such a lust for members in the Church in these modern times, that the officials and preachers have entirely lost sight of the members who have violated baptismal covenants, and who are living in open disregard of God's Word. The idea now is quantity in membership, not quality. The purity of the Church is put in the background in the craze to secure numbers, and to pad the Church rolls and make large figures in statistical columns. Prayer, much prayer, mutual prayer, would bring the Church back to Scriptural standards, and would purge the Church of many wrongdoers, while it might cure not a few of their evil lives.

Prayer and Church discipline are not new revelations of the Christian dispensation. These two things had a high place in the Jewish Church. Instances are too numerous to mention all of them. Ezra is a case in point. When he returned from the captivity, he found a sad and distressing condition of things among the Lord's people who were left in the land. They had not separated themselves from the surrounding heathen people, and had intermarried with them, contrary to Divine commands. And those high in the Church were involved, the priests and the Levites with others. Ezra was greatly moved at the account given him, and rent his garments and wept and prayed. Evil doers in the Church did not meet his approval, nor did he shut his eyes to them nor excuse them, neither did he compromise the situation. When he had finished confessing the sins of the people and his praying, the people assembled themselves before him and joined him in a covenant agreement to put away from them their evil doings, and wept and prayed in company with Ezra.

The result was that the people thoroughly repented of their transgressions, and Israel was reformed. Praying and a good man, who was neither blind nor unconcerned, did the deed.

Of Ezra it is written, "For he mourned because of the transgression of them that had been carried away." So it is with every praying man in the Church when he has eyes to see the transgression of evil doers in the Church, who has a heart to grieve over them and who has a spirit in him so concerned about the Church that he prays about it.

Blessed is that Church who has praying leaders, who can see that which is disorderly in the Church, who are grieved about it, and who put forth their hands to correct the evils which harm God's cause as a weight to its progress. One point in the indictment against those "Who are at ease in Zion," referred to by Amos, is that "they are not grieved for the affliction of Joseph." And this same indictment could be brought against Church leaders of modern times. They are not grieved because the members are engulfed in a craze for worldly, carnal things, nor when there are those in the Church walking openly in disorder, whose lives scandalise religion. Of course such leaders do not pray over the matter, for praying would beget a spirit of solicitude in them for these evil doers, and would drive away the spirit of unconcern which possesses them.

It would be well for prayerless Church leaders and careless pastors to read the account of the ink horn man in Ezekiel, 9th chapter, where God instructed the prophet to send through the city certain men who would destroy those in the city because of the great evils found therein. But certain persons were to be spared. These were they who "sigh and cry for all the abominations that be done in the midst of the city." The man with the ink horn was to mark every one of these sighers and mourners so that they would escape the impending destruction. Please note that the instructions were that the slaying of those who did not mourn and sigh should "Begin at my sanctuary."

What a lesson for non-praying, unconcerned officials of the modern Church! How few there are who "sigh and cry" for present-day abominations in the land, and who are grieved over the desolations of Zion! What need for "two or three to be gathered together" in a concert of prayer over these conditions, and in the secret place weep and pray for the sins in Zion!

This concert of prayer, this agreement in praying, taught by our Lord in the eighteenth chapter of Matthew, finds proof and illustration elsewhere. This was the kind of prayer which Paul referred to in his request to his Roman brethren, recorded in Romans 15:30:

"Now I beseech you, brethren, for the Lord Jesus Christ's sake, and for the love of the Spirit, that ye strive together with me in your prayers to God for me; that I may be delivered from them that do not believe in Judea."

Here is unity in prayer, prayer by agreement, and prayer which drives directly at deliverance from unbelieving and evil men, the same kind of prayer urged by our Lord, and the end practically the same, deliverance from unbelieving men, that deliverance wrought either by bringing them to repentance or by exclusion from the Church.

The same idea is found in 2 Thes. 3:1:

"Finally, brethren, pray for us that the word of the Lord may have free course and be glorified, even as it is with you; and that we may be delivered from unreasonable and wicked men."

Here is united prayer requested by an Apostle, among other things, for deliverance from wicked men, that same that the Church of God needs in this day. By joining their prayers to his, there was the desired end of riddance from men who were hurtful to the Church of God and who were a hindrance to the running of the Word of the Lord. Let us ask, are there not in the present-day Church those who are a positive hindrance to the on-going of the Word of the Lord? What better course is there than to jointly pray over the question, at the same time using the Christ-given course of discipline first to save them, but failing in that course, to excise them from the body?

Does that seem a harsh course? Then our Lord was guilty of harshness Himself, for He ends these directions by saying, "But if he neglect to hear the Church, let him be unto thee as a heathen man and a publican."

No more is this harshness than is the act of the skilful surgeon, who sees the whole body and its members endangered by a gangrenous limb, and severs the limb from the body for the good of the whole. No more was it harshness in the captain and crew of the vessel on which Jonah was found, when the storm arose threatening destruction to all on board, to cast the fleeing prophet overboard. What seems harshness is obedience to God, is for the welfare of the Church, and is wise in the extreme.

Chapter 12

THE UNIVERSALITY OF PRAYER

Prayer is far-reaching in its influence and world-wide in its effects. It affects all men, affects them everywhere, and affects them in all things. It touches man's interest in time and eternity. It lays hold upon God and moves Him to interfere in the affairs of earth. It moves the angels to minister to men in this life. It restrains and defeats the devil in his schemes to ruin man. Prayer goes everywhere and lays its hand upon everything. There is a universality in prayer. When we talk about prayer and its work we must use universal terms. It is individual in its application and benefits, but it is general and world-wide at the same time in its good influences. It blesses man in every event of life, furnishes him help in every emergency, and gives him comfort in every trouble. There is no experience through which man is called to go but prayer is there as a helper, a comforter and a guide.

When we speak of the universality of prayer, we discover many sides to it. First, it may be remarked that all men ought to pray. Prayer is intended for all men, because all men need God and need what God has and what prayer only can secure. As men are called upon to pray everywhere, by consequence all men must pray for men are everywhere. Universal terms are used when men are commanded to pray, while there is a promise in universal terms to all who call upon God for pardon, for mercy and for help:

"For there is no difference; for the same Lord over all is rich unto all that call upon him. For whosoever shall call upon the name of the Lord shall be saved."

As there is no difference in the state of sin in which men are found, and all men need the saving grace of God which only can bless them, and as this saving grace is obtained only in answer to prayer, therefore all men are called on to pray because of their very needs.

It is a rule of Scriptural interpretation that whenever a command issues with no limitation, it is universal in binding force. So the words of the Lord in Isaiah are to the point:

"Seek ye the Lord while he may be found; call ye upon him while he is near. Let the wicked forsake his

way, and the unrighteous man his thoughts, and let him return unto the Lord, who will have mercy, and to our God who will abundantly pardon."

So that as wickedness is universal, and as pardon is needed by all men, so all men must seek the Lord while he may be found, and must call upon Him while he is near. Prayer belongs to all men because all men are redeemed in Christ. It is a privilege for every man to pray, but it is no less a bounden duty for them to call upon God. No sinner is debarred from the mercy seat. All are welcomed to approach the throne of grace with all their wants and woes, with all their sins and burdens.

"Come all the world, come, sinner thou,
All things in Christ are ready now."

Whenever a poor sinner turns his eyes to God, no matter where he is nor what his guilt and sinfulness, the eye of God is upon him and His ear is opened to his prayers.

But men may pray everywhere, since God is accessible in every clime and under all circumstances. "I will therefore that men pray everywhere, lifting up holy hands, without wrath and doubting."

No locality is too distant from God on earth to reach heaven. No place is so remote that God cannot see and hear one who looks toward Him and seeks His face. Oliver Holden puts into a hymn these words:

> "Then, my soul, in every strait,
> To Thy Father come and wait;
> He will answer every prayer;
> God is present everywhere."

There is just this modification of the idea that one can pray everywhere. Some places, because of the evil business carried on there, or because of the environments which belong there, growing out of the place itself, the moral character of those who carry on the business, and of those who support it, are localities where prayer would not be in place. We might instance the saloon, the theatre, the opera, the card table, the dance, and other like places of worldly amusement. Prayer is so much out of place at such places that no one would ever presume to pray. Prayer would be an intrusion, so regarded by the owners, the patrons and the supporters of such places. Furthermore those who attend such places are not praying people. They belong almost entirely to the prayerless crowd of worldlings.

While we are to pray everywhere, it unquestionably means that we are not to frequent places where we cannot pray. To pray everywhere is to pray in all legitimate places, and to attend especially those places where prayer is welcome, and is given a gracious hospitality. To pray everywhere is to preserve the spirit of prayer in places of business, in our intercourse with men, and in the privacy of the home amid all of its domestic cares.

The Model Prayer of our Lord, called familiarly "The Lord's Prayer," is the universal prayer, because it is peculiarly adapted to all men everywhere in all circumstances in all times of need. It can be put in the mouths of all people in all nations, and in all times. It is a model of praying which needs no amendment nor alteration for every family, people and nation.

Furthermore, prayer has its universal application in that all men are to be the subjects of prayer. All men everywhere are to be prayed for. Prayer must take in all of Adam's fallen race because all men are fallen in Adam, redeemed in Christ, and are benefited by prayers for them. This is Paul's doctrine in his prayer directory in 1 Tim. 2:1:

"I exhort, therefore, that first of all, supplications, prayers, intercessions and giving of thanks be made for all men."

There is strong Scriptural warrant, therefore, for reaching out and embracing all men in our prayers, since not only are we commanded thus to pray for them, but the reason given is that Christ gave Himself a ransom for all men, and all men are provisionally beneficiaries of the atoning death of Jesus Christ.

But lastly, and more at length, prayer has a universal side in that all things which concern us are to be prayed about, while all things which are for our good, physical, social, intellectual, spiritual, and eternal, are subjects of prayer. Before, however, we consider this phase of prayer let us stop and again look at the universal prayer for all men. As a special class to be prayed for, we may mention those who have control in state or who bear rule in the Church. Prayer has mighty potencies. It makes good rulers, and makes them better rulers. It restrains the lawless and the despotic. Rulers are to be prayed for. They are not out of the reach and the control of prayer, because they are not out of the reach and control of God. Wicked Nero was on the throne of Rome when Paul wrote these words to Timothy urging prayer for those in authority.

Christian lips are to breathe prayers for the cruel and infamous rulers in state as well as for the righteous and the benign governors and princes. Prayer is to be as far-reaching as the race, "for all men." Humanity is to burden our hearts as we pray, and all men are to engage our thoughts in approaching a throne of grace. In our praying hours, all men must have a place. The wants and woes of the entire race are to broaden and make tender our sympathies, and inflame our petitions. No little man can pray. No man with narrow views of God, of His plan to save men, and of the universal needs of all men, can pray effectually. It takes a broad-minded man, who understands God and His purposes in the atonement, to pray well. No cynic can pray. Prayer is the divinest philanthropy, as well as giant-great-heartedness. Prayer comes from a big heart, filled with thoughts about all men and with sympathies for all men.

Prayer runs parallel with the will of God, "who will have all men to be saved and to come unto the knowledge of the truth."

Prayer reaches up to heaven, and brings heaven down to earth. Prayer has in its hands a double blessing. It rewards him who prays, and blesses him who is prayed for. It brings peace to warring passions and calms warring elements. Tranquillity is the happy fruit of true praying. There is an inner calm which comes to him who prays and an outer calm as well. Prayer creates "quiet and peaceable lives in all godliness and honesty."

Right praying not only makes life beautiful in peace, but redolent in righteousness and weighty in influence. Honesty, gravity, integrity and weight in character are the natural and essential fruits of prayer.

It is this kind of world-wide, large-hearted, unselfish praying which pleases God well, and which is acceptable in His sight, because it cooperates with His will and runs in gracious streams to all men and to each man. It is this kind of praying which the man Christ Jesus did when on earth, and the same kind which He is now doing at His Father's right hand in heaven, as our Mighty Intercessor. He is the pattern of prayer. He is between God and man, the one Mediator, who gave Himself a ransom for all men, and for each man.

So it is that true prayer links itself to the will of God, and runs in streams of solicitude, and compassion, and intercession for men. As Jesus Christ died for every one involved in the fall, so prayer girdles every one and gives itself for the benefit of every one. Like our one Mediator between God and man, he who prays stands midway between God and man, with prayers, supplications, "and strong cryings and tears." Prayer holds in its grasp the movements of the race of man, and embraces the destinies of men for all eternity. The king and the beggar are both affected by it. It touches heaven and moves earth. Prayer holds earth to heaven and brings heaven in close contact with earth.

> "Your guides and brethren bear
> Forever on your mind;
> Extend the arms of mighty prayer
> In grasping all mankind."

Chapter 13

PRAYER AND MISSIONS

Missions mean the giving of the Gospel to those of Adam's fallen race who have never heard of Christ and his atoning death. It means the giving to others the opportunity to hear of salvation through our Lord Jesus Christ, and allowing others to have a chance to receive, and accept the blessings of the Gospel, as we have it in Christianised lands. It means that those who enjoy the benefits of the Gospel give these same religious advantages and Gospel privileges to all of mankind. Prayer has a great deal to do with missions. Prayer is the hand-maid of missions. The success of all real missionary effort is dependent on prayer. The life and spirit of missions are the life and spirit of prayer. Both prayer and missions were born in the Divine Mind. Prayer and missions are bosom companions. Prayer creates and makes missions successful, while missions lean heavily on prayer. In Psalm 72, one which deals with the Messiah, it is stated that "prayer shall be made for him continually." Prayer would be made for His coming to save man, and prayer would be made for the success of the plan of salvation which He would come to set on foot.

The Spirit of Jesus Christ is the spirit of missions. Our Lord Jesus Christ was Himself the first missionary. His promise and advent composed the first missionary movement. The missionary spirit is not simply a phase of the Gospel, not a mere feature of the plan of salvation, but is its very spirit and life. The missionary movement is the Church of Jesus Christ marching in militant array, with the design of possessing the whole world of mankind for Christ. Whoever is touched by the Spirit of God is fired by the missionary spirit. An anti-missionary Christian is a contradiction in terms. We might say that it would be impossible to be an anti-missionary Christian because of the impossibility for the Divine and human forces to put men in such a state as not to align them with the missionary cause. Missionary impulse is the heart-beat of our Lord Jesus Christ, sending the vital forces of Himself through the whole body of the Church. The spiritual life of God's people rises or falls with the force of those heart-beats. When these life forces cease, then death ensues. So that anti-missionary Churches are dead Churches, just as anti-missionary Christians are dead Christians.

The craftiest wile of Satan, if he cannot prevent a great movement for God, is to debauch the movement. If he can put the movement first, and the spirit of the movement in the background, he has materialised and thoroughly debauched the movement. Mighty prayer only will save the movement from being materialised, and keep the spirit of the movement strong and controlling.

The key of all missionary success is prayer. That key is in the hands of the home churches. The trophies won by our Lord in heathen lands will be won by praying missionaries, not by professional workers in foreign lands. More especially will this success be won by saintly praying in the churches at home. The home church on her knees fasting and praying, is the great base of spiritual supplies, the sinews of war, and the pledge of victory in this dire and final conflict. Financial resources are not the real sinews of war in this fight. Machinery in itself carries no power to break down heathen walls, open effectual doors and win heathen hearts to Christ. Prayer alone can do the deed.

Aaron and Hur did not more surely give victory to Israel through Moses, than a praying church through Jesus Christ will give victory on every battlefield in heathen lands. It is as true in foreign fields as it is in home lands. The praying church wins the contest. The home church has done but a paltry thing when she has furnished the money to establish missions and support her missionaries. Money is important, but money without prayer is powerless in the face of the darkness, the wretchedness and the sin in unchristianised lands. Prayerless giving breeds barrenness and death. Poor praying at home is the solution of poor results in the foreign field. Prayerless giving is the secret of all crises in the missionary movements of the day, and is the occasion of the accumulation of debts in missionary boards.

It is all right to urge men to give of their means to the missionary cause. But it is much more important to urge them to give their prayers to the movement. Foreign missions need, today, more the power of prayer than the power of money. Prayer can make even poverty in the missionary cause move on amidst difficulties and hindrances. Much money without prayer is helpless and powerless in the face of the utter darkness and sin and wretchedness on the foreign field.

This is peculiarly a missionary age. Protestant Christianity is stirred as it never was before in the line of aggression in pagan lands. The missionary movement has taken on proportions that awaken hope, kindle enthusiasm, and which demand the attention, if not the interest, of the coldest and the most lifeless. Nearly every Church has caught the contagion, and the sails of their proposed missionary movements are spread wide to catch the favouring breezes. Herein is the danger just now, that the missionary movement will go ahead of the missionary spirit. This has always been the peril of the Church, losing the substance in the shade, losing the spirit in the outward shell, and contenting itself in the mere parade of the movement, putting the force of effort in the movement and not in the spirit.

The magnificence of this movement may not only blind us to the spirit of it, but the spirit which should give life and shape to the movement may be lost in the wealth of the movement as the ship, borne by favouring winds, may be lost when these winds swell to a storm.

Not a few of us have heard eloquent and earnest speeches stressing the imperative need of money for missions where we have heard one stressing the imperative need of prayer. All our plans and devices drive to the one end of raising money, not to quicken faith and promote prayer. The common idea among Church leaders is that if we get the money, prayer will come as a matter of course. The very reverse is the truth. If we get the Church at the business of praying, and thus secure the spirit of missions, money will more than likely come as a matter of course. Spiritual agencies and spiritual forces never come as a matter of course. Spiritual duties and spiritual factors, left to the "matter of course" law, will surely fall out and die. Only the things which are stressed live and rule in the spiritual realm. They who give, will not necessarily pray. Many in our churches are liberal givers who are noted for their prayerlessness. One of the evils of the present-day missionary movement lies just there. Giving is entirely removed from prayer. Prayer receives scant attention, while giving stands out prominently. They who truly pray will be moved to give. Praying creates the giving spirit. The praying ones will give liberally and self-denyingly. He who enters his closet to God, will also open his purse to God. But perfunctory, grudging, assessment-giving kills the very spirit of prayer. Emphasising the material to the neglect of the spiritual, by an inexorable law retires and discounts the spiritual.

It is truly wonderful how great a part money plays in the modern religious movements, and how little prayer plays in them. In striking contrast with that statement, it is marvellous how little part money played in primitive Christianity as a factor in spreading the Gospel, and how wonderful part prayer played in it.

The grace of giving is nowhere cultured to a richer growth than in the closet. If all our missionary boards and secretaryships were turned into praying bands, until the agony of real prayer and travail with Christ for a perishing world came on them, real estate, bank stocks, United States bonds would be in the market for the spreading of Christ's Gospel among men. If the spirit of prayer prevailed, missionary boards whose individual members are worth millions, would not be staggering under a load of debt and great Churches would not have a yearly deficit and a yearly grumbling, grudging, and pressure to pay a beggarly assessment to support a mere handful of missionaries, with the additional humiliation of debating the question of recalling some of them. The on-going of Christ's kingdom is locked up in the closet of prayer by Christ Himself, and not in the contribution box.

The Prophet Isaiah, looking down the centuries with the vision of a seer, thus expresses his purpose to continue in prayer and give God no rest till Christ's kingdom be established among men:

"For Zion's sake will I not hold my peace, and for Jerusalem's sake I will not rest till the righteousness thereof goeth forth as brightness, and the salvation thereof as a lamp that burneth."

Then, foretelling the final success of the Christian Church, he thus speaks:

"And the Gentiles shall see thy righteousness, and all kings thy glory, and thou shalt be called by a new name, which the mouth of the Lord shall name."

Then the Lord, Himself, by the mouth of this Evangelical prophet, declares as follows:

"I have set watchmen upon thy walls, O Jerusalem, which shall never hold their peace, day nor night. Ye that make mention of the Lord, keep not silence. And give him no rest till he establish and till he make Jerusalem a praise in the earth."

In the margin of our Bible, it reads, "Ye that are the Lord's remembrancers." The idea is, that these praying ones are those who are the Lord's remembrancers, those who remind Him of what He has promised, and who give Him no rest till God's Church is established in the earth.

And one of the leading petitions in the Lord's Prayer deals with this same question of the establishing of God's kingdom and the progress of the Gospel in the short, pointed petition, "Thy kingdom come," with the added words, "Thy will be done on earth as it is done in heaven."

The missionary movement in the Apostolic Church was born in an atmosphere of fasting and prayer. The very movement looking to offering the blessings of the Christian Church to the Gentiles was on the housetop on the occasion when Peter went up there to pray, and God showed him His Divine purpose to extend the privileges of the Gospel to the Gentiles, and to break down the middle wall of partition between Jew and Gentile.

But more specifically Paul and Barnabas were

definitely called and set apart to the missionary field at Antioch when the Church there had fasted and prayed. It was then the Holy Spirit answered from heaven: "Separate me Barnabas and Saul for the work whereunto I have called them."

Please note this was not the call to the ministry of Paul and Barnabas, but more particularly their definite call to the foreign field. Paul had been called to the ministry years before this, even at his conversion. This was a subsequent call to a work born of special and continued prayer in the Church at Antioch. God calls men not only to the ministry but to be missionaries. Missionary work is God's work. And it is the God-called men who are to do it. These are the kind of missionaries which have wrought well and successfully in the foreign field in the past, and the same kind will do the work in the future, or it will not be done.

It is praying missionaries who are needed for the work, and it is a praying church who sends them out, which are prophecies of the success which is promised. The sort of religion to be exported by missionaries is of the praying sort. The religion to which the heathen world is to be converted is a religion of prayer, and a religion of prayer to the true God. The heathen world already prays to its idols and false gods. But they are to be taught by praying missionaries, sent out by a praying Church, to cast away their idols and to begin to call upon the name of the Lord Jesus Christ. No prayerless church can transport to heathen lands a praying religion. No prayerless missionary can bring heathen idolaters who know not our God to their knees to true prayer until he becomes pre-eminently a man of prayer. As it takes praying men at home to do God's work, none the less does it take praying missionaries to bring those who sit in darkness to the light.

The most noted and most successful missionaries have been pre-eminently men of prayer. David Livingstone, William Taylor, Adoniram Judson, Henry Martyn, and Hudson Taylor, with many more, form a band of illustrious praying men whose impress and influence still abide where they laboured. No prayerless man is wanted for this job. Above everything else, the primary qualification for every missionary is prayer. Let him be, above everything else, a man of prayer. And when the crowning day comes, and the records are made up and read at the great judgment day, then it will appear how well praying men wrought in the hard fields of heathendom, and how much was due to them in laying the foundations of Christianity in those fields.

The one only condition which is to give worldwide power to this Gospel is prayer, and the spread of this Gospel will depend on prayer. The energy which was to give it marvelous momentum and conquering power over all its malignant and powerful foes is the energy of prayer.

The fortunes of the kingdom of Jesus Christ are not made by the feebleness of its foes. They are strong and bitter and have ever been strong, and ever will be. But mighty prayer—this is the one great spiritual force which will enable the Lord Jesus Christ to enter into full possession of His kingdom, and secure for Him the heathen as His inheritance, and the uttermost part of the earth for His possession.

It is prayer which will enable Him to break His foes with a rod of iron, that will make these foes tremble in their pride and power, who are but frail potter's vessels, to be broken in pieces by one stroke of His hand. A person who can pray is the mightiest instrument Christ has in this world. A praying Church is stronger than all the gates of hell.

God's decree for the glory of His Son's kingdom is dependent on prayer for its fulfilment: "Ask of me, and I will give thee the heathen for thy inheritance, and the uttermost part of the earth for thy possession." God the Father gives nothing to His Son only through prayer. And the reason why the Church has not received more in the missionary work in which it is engaged is the lack of prayer. "Ye have not, because ye ask not."

Every dispensation foreshadowing the coming of Christ when the world has been evangelised, at the end of time, rests upon these constitutional provisions, God's decree, His promises and prayer.

However far away that day of victory by distance or time, or remoteness of shadowy type, prayer is the essential condition on which the dispensation becomes strong, typical and representative. From Abraham, the first of the nation of the Israelites, the friend of God, down to this dispensation of the Holy Spirit, this has been true.

> "The nations call! From sea to sea
> Extends the thrilling cry,
> 'Come over, Christians, if there be,
> And help us, ere we die.'
> "Our hearts, O Lord, the summons
> feel;
> Let hand with heart combine,
> And answer to the world's appeal,
> By giving 'that is thine.'"

Our Lord's plan for securing workers in the foreign missionary field is the same plan He set on foot for obtaining preachers. It is by the process of praying. It is the prayer plan as distinguished from all man-made plans. These mission workers are to be "sent men." God must send them. They are God-called, divinely moved to this great work. They are inwardly moved to enter the harvest fields of the world and gather sheaves for the heavenly garners. Men do not choose to be missionaries any more than they choose to be preachers. God sends out labourers in His harvest field in answer to the prayers of His church. Here is the Divine plan as set forth by our Lord:

"But when he saw the multitudes, he was moved with compassion on them, because they fainted, and were as sheep having no shepherd. Then saith he unto his disciples, The harvest truly is plenteous, but the labourers are few. Pray ye, therefore, the Lord of the harvest that he will send forth labourers into his harvest."

It is the business of the home church to do the praying. It is the Lord's business to call and send forth the labourers. The Lord does not do the praying. The Church does not do the calling. And just as our Lord's compassions were aroused by the sight of multitudes, weary, hungry, and scattered, exposed to evils, as sheep having no shepherd, so whenever the Church has eyes to see the vast multitudes of earth's inhabitants, descendants of Adam, weary in soul, living in darkness, and wretched and sinful, will it be moved to compassion, and begin to pray the Lord of the harvest to send forth labourers into His harvest.

Missionaries, like ministers, are born of praying people. A praying church begets labourers in the harvest-field of the world. The scarcity of missionaries argues a non-praying church. It is all right to send trained men to the foreign field, but first of all they must be God-sent. The sending is the fruit of prayer. As praying men are the occasion of sending them, so in turn the workers must be praying men. And the prime mission of these praying missionaries is to convert prayerless heathen men into praying men. Prayer is the proof of their calling, their Divine credentials, and their work.

He who is not a praying man at home needs the one fitness to become a mission worker abroad. He who has not the spirit which moves him toward sinners at home, will hardly have a spirit of compassion for sinners abroad. Missionaries are not made of men who are failures at home. He who will be a man of prayer abroad must, before anything else, be a man of prayer in his home church. If he be not engaged in turning sinners away from their prayerless ways at home, he will hardly succeed in turning away the heathen from their prayerless ways. In other words, it takes the same spiritual qualifications for being a home worker as it does for being a foreign worker.

God in His own way, in answer to the prayers of His Church, calls men into His harvest-fields. Sad will be the day when Missionary Boards and Churches overlook that fundamental fact, and send out their own chosen men independent of God.

Is the harvest great? Are the labourers few? Then "pray ye the Lord of the harvest to send forth labourers into his harvest." Oh, that a great wave of prayer would sweep over the Church asking God to send out a great army of labourers into the needy harvest fields of the earth! No danger of the Lord of the harvest sending out too many labourers and crowding the fields. He who calls will most certainly provide the means for supporting those whom He calls and sends forth.

The one great need in the modern missionary movement is intercessors. They were scarce in the days of Isaiah. This was his complaint:

"And he saw that there was no man, and wondered that there was no intercessor."

So today there is great need of intercessors, first, for the needy harvest-fields of earth, born of a Christly compassion for the thousands without the Gospel; and then intercessors for labourers to be sent forth by God into the needy fields of earth.